Selection
Michael Dorrian
Liz Farrelly

Art Direction
Michael Dorrian

Words
Liz Farrelly

Design
Lee Owens

Thanks to
Alex Acosta_ Rex Advincula_
Marc Atkinson_ David Azurdia_
David Bailey_ Clemens
Baldermann_ Stefanie Barth_ Algy
Batten_ Alex Bec_ Blackbooks_
Ric Blackshaw_ Simon Blackwell_
Edwina Blasdale_ Phil Bold_
Sarah Boris_ Despina Bournele_
Anne Brassier_ Stefan G. Bucher_
Peter Bünnagel_ Reed Burgoyne_
Alison Carmichael_ Mike Carney_
Patrick Carvalho Dumont_ Chin-
Lien Chen_ Jan Christensen_
Susanna Cook_ Peter Crnokrak_
Julien Crouïgneau_ Mike Curtis_
Rosa de Jong_ Carter Delmont_
Sergio del Puerto_ Mark Denton_
Mark Dormand_ Patrick Duffy_
Brendan Elliott_ Anna Euklund_
Guto Evans_ Jessie Farweather_
Julien Gendre_ Götz Gramlich_
Peter Gray_ Sam Green_ Johannes
Grimmond_ Peter Grundy_ Sam
Harris_ Kelly Hartman_ Richard
Hogg_ Richard Hunt_ Diego
Hurtado de Mendoza_ Agathe
Jacquillat_ Tim Jeffrey_ Jewboy
Corp_ Nick Jones_ Mike Kelar_
Matt Kelley_ Erika Kim_ Barbara
Kotte_ Denis Kovac_ Adam
Larson_ Morten Laursen_ Diane

Christian Montenegro_ Jarrik
Muller_ Martijn Oostra_ Stephen
Owen_ Quam Payne_ Joanna
Pearce_ Peter + Paul_ Richard
Pijs_ Angelique Piliere_ Vic
Polkinghorne_ Celeste Prevost_
Anne-Lene Prof_ Rex+Joyce_
Cybu Richli_ Tim Schmitt_ Frank
Schouwaerts_ Natasha Shah_
Steve Sims_ Andy Smith_ Mark
Smith_ Matt Smith_ Rose Stallard_
Astrid Stavro_ Nick Steel_ Keith
Stephenson_ Jakob Straub_
Jernej Stritar_ Joseph Sung_
Gemma Tabb_ Joyce Tai_ Olivia
Triggs_ Therese Vandling_ Gregg
Virostek_ Chris Vermaas_ Giulio
Vesprini_ Tomi Vollauschek_
Omar Vulpinari_ Simone
Wagener_ Geoff Wagner_ Jame
Waterhouse_ Damien Weighill_
David Weik_ Bianca Wendt_
Lonne Wennekendonk_ Daniel
Westwood_ Matt Wheatcroft_
Darren Whittingham_ Matt Willey_
Steve Wilson_ Matt Wingfield_
Clien Wintzen_ Giles Woodward_
Ellen Zhao_

Whether working within the usual restrictions of size, format and budget, or thinking completely outside the box to create a business card from wood, metal, plastic or any other combination of unusual materials and techniques, designing a business card is about embodying an idea, a personality or a concept; it's not simply a means of purveying basic information.

This collection of business cards – our third look at an ever-evolving genre – rounds up another bunch of the most innovative and arresting examples in circulation today, and goes to prove, yet again, just how versatile and evocative these humble graphic iterations can be.

Now that we have mobile phones and hand-held devices capable of storing hundreds of names and contact details, what's the point of having a business card? Why hand out an arcane scrap of printed matter when a simple text message will instantly log your name and number in another's phone? In an age that has mobile computing at its fingertips, isn't a business card, well, a little old-fashioned?

If that's your attitude, then you're missing the point, and a trick... Witness The Joker, in the latest Batman escapade, "The Dark Knight". His signature calling card crops up again and again: delivered to an intended victim; exploding out of a flaming car; marking the scene of a crime. "Here's my card," he says nonchalantly to the assembled villains of Gotham City, underlining that he means business. The Joker's 'playing card' functions much like any other business card; it may or may not depict his phone number (too big a clue!), but it does provide an insight into both his warped personality and devilish intentions. Think of the business card as a snapshot of your "self", and the true design potential becomes obvious.

The cards are sourced from a wide range of professional designers, illustrators and photographers, as well as creative amateurs, from right around the world – you don't have to be a graphic designer to make your own card. Try out the online card-printing resources and showcase your range of work, as Diane Leyman, the creator of Notes accessories, does. And designers themselves don't necessarily go for the traditional print-on-paper model. Be like Frederique Daubal (see p.256) and simply pick up a pen to make a mark – on anything – delivering a fully customized, unique message to each and every recipient.

What we've noticed with this selection, though, is that graphic designers are achieving show-stopping results, even with the most straightforward of means, starting with black ink on white card. Others are exploring the widest possibilities of print technology and exploiting the medium to the max by specifying spot-colour, foil, varnish, embossing, die-cutting and folding. To that end, all sorts of imagery – type, logo, photograph, illustration and pattern – is being realized in the most innovative manner.

Design
Diane Leyman

For
Notes_
Handmade
Accessories_
Brighton, UK

Info
Using photos of a selection of her hand-made bags and purses, Diane Leyman made these mini business cards with the help of moo.com. Moo-cards are popular with the crafting community, as they allow makers to showcase a range of objects, are printed on sustainable card stock, and are cute and affordable.

is to design a card that never becomes obsolete, and that will accommodate new contact details when you move studio. Or keep the information simple – one URL, one phone number... Freelance designer Jane Waterhouse is currently travelling, working and living in new places, so her business card reflects that; cut and fold it into a mini-globe for your desk and contact her any time, any place, via the Internet.

A recent scheme to offset carbon emissions from the design industry saw US paper manufacturer, NewPage, plant a tree for every business card collected from graphic design delegates at the national conference of the American Institute for Graphic Arts (AIGA). Share your contact details and help the planet breathe. Now, how could you do that without a business card?

Add to the mix another element, the tactile quality of unusual stocks or materials, which may be recycled or re-purposed, pre-printed or found, and the humble business card becomes an even more palpable manifestation of an individual or business. It's instantly memorable simply because it feels "different". An out-of-the-ordinary business card will act as an invaluable aide-mémoire, reminding a new contact that a certain laser-cut, plywood rendition belongs to an intriguing 3D designer, aka Betham Wood (see pp. 248–249).

Of course, there is the ecological impact with having an "actual" card to consider. More graphic design requires that more paper be manufactured, more trees cut down and processed, and more waste produced. One way around this real-world conundrum

NO PERMANENT ADDRESS.

Jane Waterhouse | Graphic Designer | www.janewaterhouseglobal.com

Design
Jane Waterhouse

For
Jane Waterhouse_
Designer_
Global

Info
This freelance designer is on a round-the-world trip; her card may be cut and folded into a globe.

If you could

'make someone smile'

'go everywhere, do everything'

'never come down'

'go back and do it all again'

'memento mori'

'find the one'

'try something new'

'put the world back together'

Info
The idea was to ask a roll-call of image-makers, at various stages in their careers, to illustrate their response to the question "If you could do anything tomorrow, what would it be?" The answers ranged from playful to profound, and have been compiled into a series of limited-edition prints and publications. A set of eight business cards illustrates a variety of responses and shows how just one line can spark the imagination.

For
If You Could_
Designers,
London, UK

Design
Alex Bec_
Will Hudson_
If You Could

ALFA
SIERRA
TANGO
ROMEO
INDIA
DELTA

SIERRA
TANGO
ALFA
VICTOR
ROMEO
OSCAR

Astrid Stavro

Baixada de Viladecols 3, 1º 2ª
08002 Barcelona
+34 620 550 515
astrid@astridstavro.com
www.astridstavro.com

AMÉRICA
SANTIAGO
TORONTO
ROMA
ITALIA
DINAMARCA

SANTIAGO
TORONTO
AMÉRICA
VENEZUELA
ROMA
ONTARIO

Design
Astrid Stavro_
Ana Domínguez

For
Astrid Stavro_
Designer_
Barcelona, Spain

Info
Featuring the English and Spanish versions of the radiotelephony alphabet, Astrid Stavro spells out her hard-to-pronounce name on her business card, for international clients.

+measure

Second Floor
65 Margaret Street
London W1W 8SP

Skype measuredesign
Online www.measuredesign.co.uk

Simon Blackwell
simon.blackwell@measuredesign.co.uk
+44 (0)7768 56 20 58

Info
A clever crop, and a company name is transformed into "me", a personal introduction.

For
Measure_
Designer_
London, UK

Design
Simon Blackwell_
Measure

AHOI

SCROLLAN
AM BAUMWALL

PETER BÜNNAGEL
SCROLLAN
WINSSTRASSE 32, VORDERHAUS
WIE GEHT'S

BARBARA KOTTE
SCROLLAN
WINSSTRASSE 32, VORDERHAUS
10405 BERLIN
BIS BALD

SCROLLAN
WINSSTRASSE 32, VOI
10405 BERLIN
GUTEN TAG

ANNE-LENE PROFF
SCROLLAN
HALLO

Design
Peter Bünnagel_
Barbara Kotte_
Anne-Lene Proff_
Iris Fussenegger_
Scrollan

For
Scrollan_
Designers_
Berlin, Germany

Info
A series of folded cards, printed with three overlaid spot colours to
create subtle emphases in the text, presents a welcoming attitude
by using various "hello" phrases.

Design
Matthew Wheatcroft_
Kay McKeon_
Judge Gill

For
Judge Gill_
Environmental
Designers_
Manchester, UK

Info
Judge Gill's set of business cards reflects the studio's approach, which applies sound design principles to create experiential retail environments. Using white foil and debossing on a matt black card stock, the result is tactile yet high profile, classic yet contemporary.

Judge Gill
Kevin Gill

Judge Gill
Jamie O'Donnell

Judge Gill
Chris Britton

Judge Gill
Ric Mather

Judge Gill
Rob MacKenzie

Judge Gill
Ben Barton

Judge
Gill David

Judge
Gill Claire
Duffy

Judge
Gill Matt

3 Cobourg Street
Manchester M1 3GY

Telephone
+44(0)161 228 3066
Facsimile
+44(0)161 228 0137
Email
matt.wheatcroft@judgegill.co.uk

www.judgegill.co.uk

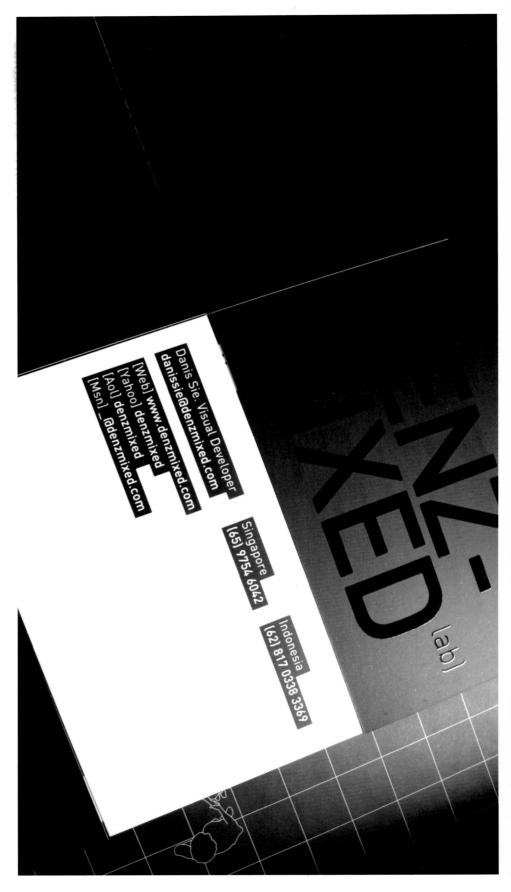

Design
Danis Sie_
Denzmixed

For
Denzmixed_
Designer_
Singapore/
Indonesia

Info
Danis Sie's definition of a business card – "simple and
straightforward, showcasing information and personality"
– is perfectly realized in his own, which uses just one colour
and a spot UV varnish.

Danis Sie. Visual Developer
danissie@denzmixed.com

[Web] www.denzmixed.com
[Yahoo] denzmixed
[Aol] denzmixed
[Msn] _@denzmixed.com

Singapore
(65) 9754 6042

Indonesia
(62) 817 0338 3369

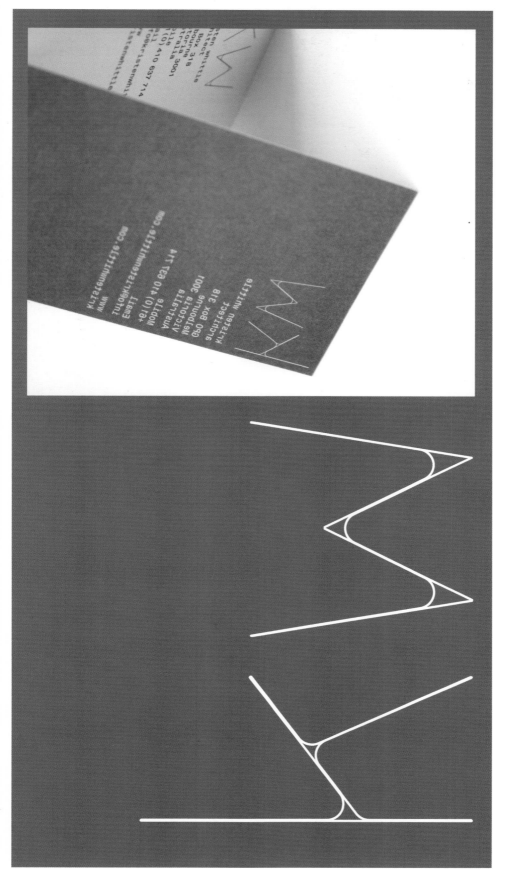

Info
Part of a larger identity programme for this innovative architect.
David Bennett's business cards for Kristen Whittle feature cleverly
constructed letterforms using lines, angles and curves that echo
the precision of architectural drawings.

For
Kristen Whittle_
Architect,
Melbourne,
Australia

Design
David Bennett_
This Studio

Design
Steven Wilson

For
Steven Wilson_
Illustrator_
Brighton, UK

Info
A virtuoso illustrator with a passion for drawing expressive representations of letterforms and words. Steven Wilson re-purposes commissioned images into an evolving series of collectable business cards.

Steven Wilson
www.wilson2000.com
steve@wilson2000.com
+44 (0)7939 216666

Steven Wilson
www.wilson2000.com
steve@wilson2000.com
+44 (0)7939 216666

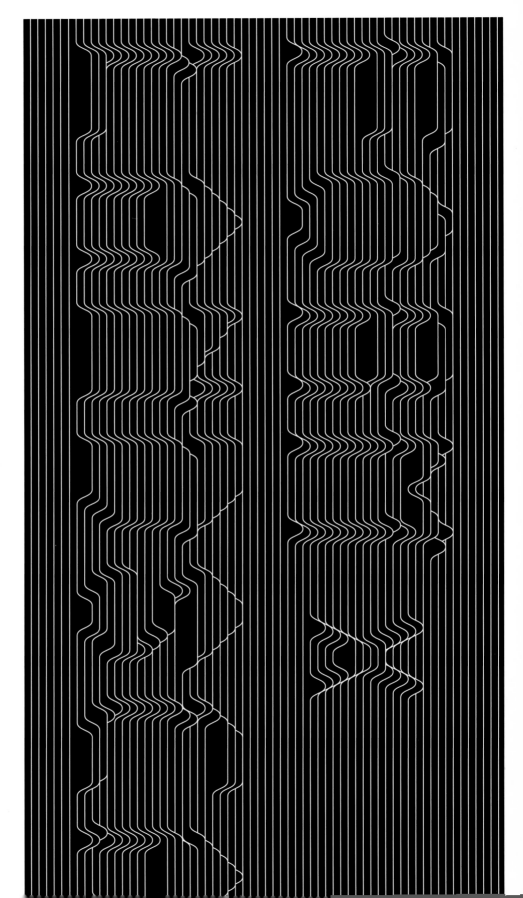

<u>Design</u>
Jessie Fairweather_
Foundry

<u>For</u>
Times Two
Architects,
Architecture
Practice_
Castlemaine,
Australia

<u>Info</u>
A landscape of white lines on a black ground has been used to create a logo, with words being formed from small deviations in the direction of the lines.

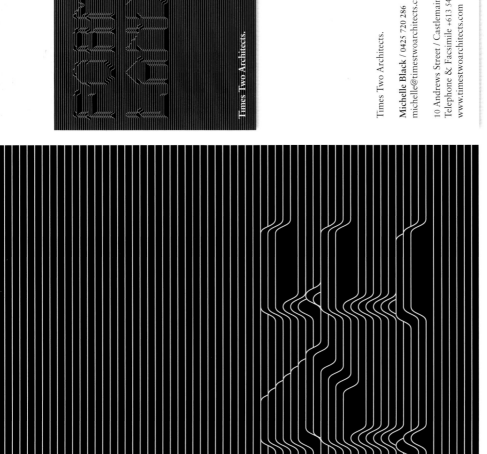

Times Two Architects.

Michelle Black / 0425 720 286
michelle@timestwoarchitects.com

10 Andrews Street / Castlemaine VIC 3450 / Australia
Telephone & Facsimile +613 5472 2213
www.timestwoarchitects.com

VONSUNG.COM

JOSEPH@VONSUNG.COM
WHITECHAPEL
DEPOT 51 CARI
LLON COURT 41
GREATOREX ST.
LONDON E1 5EN
M:44.784.349
.8177 0:44.
207.
375
.10
58

CREATIVE DIRECTOR

Design
Joseph Sung_
Vonsung

For
Vonsung_
Designers_
London, UK

Info
Practising what they preach, Vonsung go through a rebranding every season, this yellow business card being part of their Spring 'Easter Egg' edition. Yellow is about happiness, peace and highlighter pens. It's also rebellious: fast cars drive on the yellow traffic light. This set features each staff member posing in the limelight!

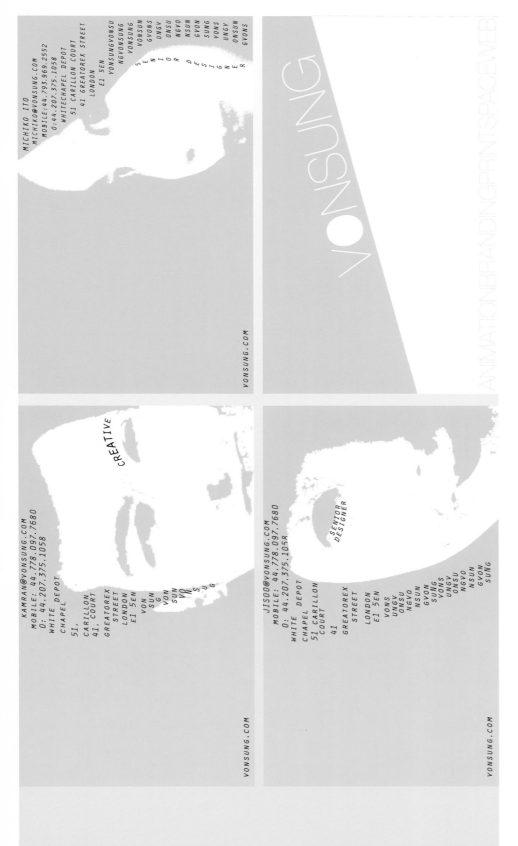

VONSUNG

ANIMATIONBRANDINGPRINTSPACEWEB

VONSUNG.COM

MICHIKO ITO
MICHIKO@VONSUNG.COM
MOBILE:44.793.969.2552
O:44.207.375.1058
WHITECHAPEL DEPOT
51 CARILLON COURT
41 GREATOREX STREET
LONDON
E1 5EN
VONSUNGVONSU
NGVONSUNG
VONSUNG
VONSUN
GVONS
UNGV
ONSU
NGVO
NSUN
GVON
SUNG
VONS
UNGV
ONSUN
GVONS

KAMRAN@VONSUNG.COM
MOBILE: 44.778.097.7680
O: 44.207.375.1058
WHITE DEPOT
CHAPEL
51.
CARILLON
41 COURT
GREATOREX
STREET
LONDON
E1 5EN
VON
SUN
G
VON
SUN
VO
S
U
G

CREATIVE

VONSUNG.COM

JISOO@VONSUNG.COM
MOBILE: 44.778.097.7680
O: 44.207.375.1058
WHITE DEPOT
CHAPEL
51 CARILLON
COURT
41
GREATOREX
STREET
LONDON
E1 5EN
VONS
UNGV
ONSU
NGVO
NSUN
GVON
SUNG
VONS
UNGV
ONSU
NGVO
NSUN
GVON
SUNG

SENIOR
DESIGNER

VONSUNG.COM

I opened
my heart
and a bird
flew in

look
pameijer

Hans Kröber

CEO

P.O. Box 22406
3003 DK Rotterdam
the Netherlands
office:
Crooswijksesingel 66
3034 CJ Rotterdam

t: 0031 10 271 00 00
f: 0031 10 271 03 10
hans.krober@pameijer.nl
www.pameijer.nl

the most
beautiful
music is
laughter

one
and all
pameijer

Jan Alblas MHA

managing director

P.O. Box 22406
3003 DK Rotterdam
the Netherlands
office:
Crooswijksesingel 66
3034 CJ Rotterdam

t: 0031 10 271 00 00
f: 0031 10 271 03 10
jan.alblas@pameijer.nl
www.pameijer.nl

Design
Studio Lonne
Wennekendonk

For
Pameijer_
Patient
Support Group_
Rotterdam, the
Netherlands

Info
This set of business cards features inspiring copywriting that
elaborates on the calligraphic elements of the organization's logo;
the eight versions of the logo highlight the partnership between
patients and carers.

like you

pameijer

P.O. Box 22406
3003 DK Rotterdam
the Netherlands
office:
Crooswijksesingel 66
3034 CJ Rotterdam

Suzanne Labots
communications advice

t: 0031 10 271 00 00
f: 0031 10 271 03 10
suzanne.labots@pameijer.nl
www.pameijer.nl

water your dreams and watch them grow

Side by Side

pameijer

P.O. Box 22406
3003 DK Rotterdam
the Netherlands
office:
Crooswijksesingel 66
3034 CJ Rotterdam

Caroline Dietzel
communications advice

t: 0031 10 271 00 00
f: 0031 10 271 03 10
caroline.dietzel@pameijer.nl
www.pameijer.nl

I winked at the moon and the moon winked back

dear cher ~~chère~~

i love j'adore

Jean-Pierre

i'd like to je voudrais bien

visit your drawing

Visit your Studio

please write to me at écris-moi à ellen@buro-gds.com

call me at appelle-moi au

+33 (0)6 72 20 32 89 or ou +1 718 478 3364

see the site regarde le site buro-gds.com

dear cher chère

i love j'adore

i'd like to je voudrais bien

please write to me at écris-moi à **ellen.zhao@web.de**

call me at appelle-moi au

+33 (0)6 72 20 32 89 or ou **+1 718 478 3364**

see the site regarde le site **buro-gds.com**

---

dear cher chère

Antoine

i love j'adore

tes chaussures

i'd like to je voudrais bien

voir R.B. avec toi

please write to me at écris-moi à **ellen.zhao@web.de**

call me at appelle-moi au

+33 (0)6 72 20 32 89 or ou **+1 718 478 3364**

see the site regarde le site **buro-gds.com**

---

dear cher chère

Pauline

i love j'adore

les lapins roses

i'd like to je voudrais bien

manger des tajines avec toi

please write to me at écris-moi à **ellen.zhao@web.de**

call me at appelle-moi au

+33 (0)6 72 20 32 89 or ou **+1 718 478 3364**

see the site regarde le site **buro-gds.com**

ELLEN ZHAO

Design
Ellen Tongzhou
Zhao_
BURO-GDS

For
BURO-GDS_
Designer_
New York, USA

Info
Designed when Ellen Tongzhou Zhao lived in Paris, this business card was a deliberate attempt at bridging the gap between individuals; the process of giving and receiving contact details is made more personal 'and flirtatious', as the French text uses the informal form of you, toi'. A smaller format than the norm was used so that the card easily fits in a wallet.

WWW.CUT-UP.CO.UK

Jo HoGAN

CREATIVE TYPO/GRAPHICS

☎:07980551117

INFO@CUT-UP.CO.UK

CUT-UP DESIGN

Design_
Jo Hogan_
Cut-Up Design

For
Cut-Up Design_
Designer/
Typographer_
London, UK

Info
Hogan combines "hand and computer" by means of various techniques and tools, including rubber stamps, assembled text, scanned objects, Xerox and Photoshop. She calls the resulting aesthetic "blade and bitmap", as seen in this example from an ongoing series of promotional business cards.

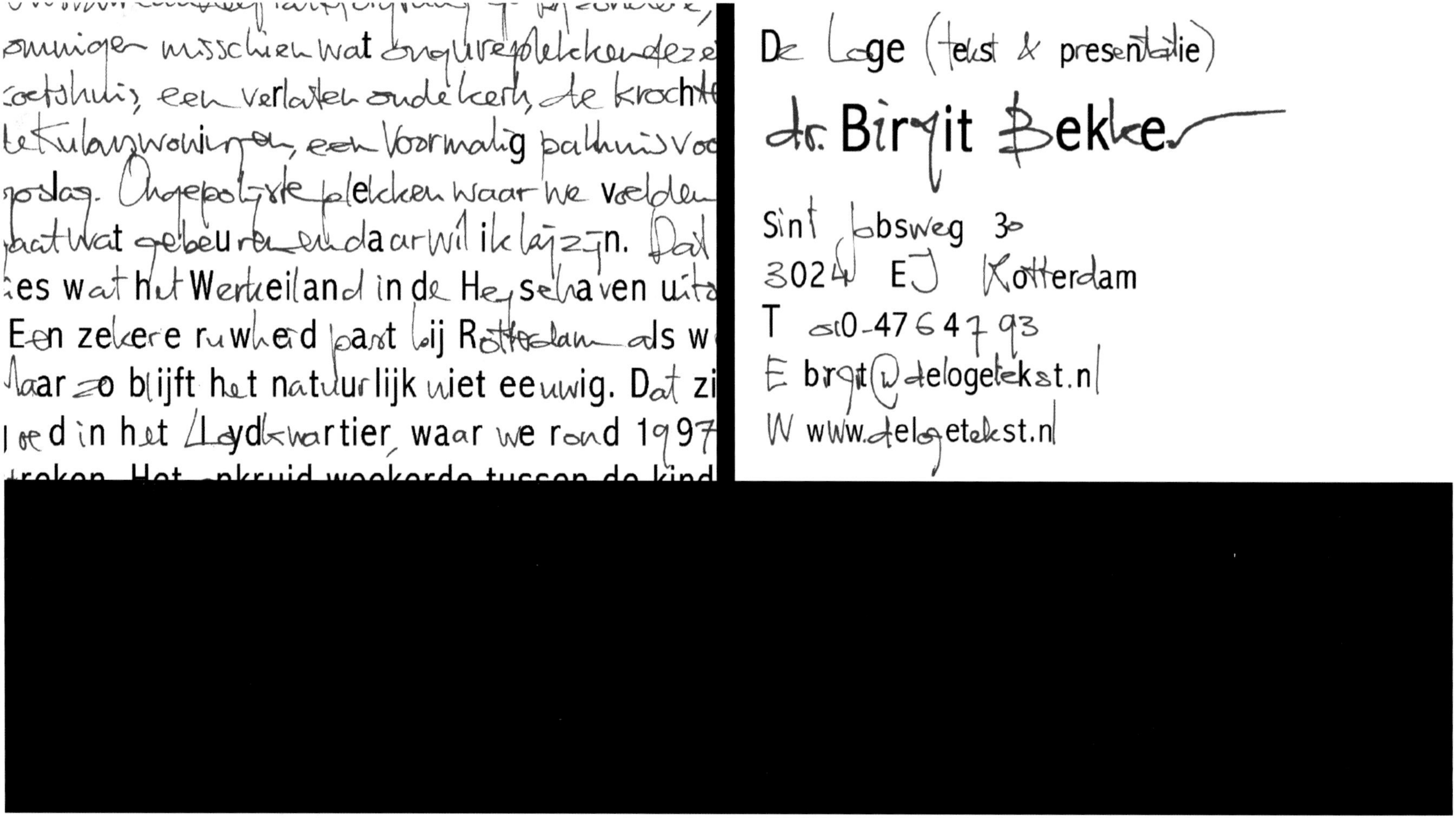

De Loge (tekst & presentatie)

dé. **Birgit Bekker**

Sint Jobsweg 30
3024 EJ Rotterdam
T 010-47 64 7 93
E brgt@delogetekst.nl
W www.delogetekst.nl

[handwritten Dutch text, partially legible]

...omuioge misschien wat ...overdreven... ...gebeurtenis... ...ze...
...oothuis; een verlaten ...de keerts, de kracht...
...tekulangwovin... ...een voormalig pakhuis voo...
...das. Onze politie plekken waar we voelen...
...wat ...bleeft... daar wil ik laj zijn. Dat...
...ies wat het Wertteiland in de Heyselhaven uit...
Een zekere ruwheid part bij Rotterdam als we...
haar zo blijft het natuurlijk niet eeuwig. Dat zi...
...d in het Lloydkvartier, waar we rond 197...

Design
Studio Lonne
Wennekendonk

For
De Loge (Tekst en
Presentatie)_
Writer_
Rotterdam,
the Netherlands

Info
Mixing the tools of the trade, this business card features two
methods of communicating; the immediacy of handwriting filling
the gaps between fragments of reproduced type. The end result
demonstrates the evolution of this writer's words, from her pen to
the printed page.

Jan Christensen

Snipetorpgata 27
3715 Skien
Norway

jan_b_christensen@yahoo.com
www.janchristensen.org

Holzmarktstr. 73
10179 Berlin
Germany

Mobile, Norway	+ 47	938 66 070
Mobile, Sweden	+ 46	768 61 35 25
Mobile, Germany	+ 49	173 176 94 24
Telephone, Germany	+ 49	30 278 90 433

Design
Jan Christensen_
Kunimoto

For
Jan Christensen_
Artist/Designer_
Berlin, Germany

Info
Entitled "You Left Some Notes", this business card reveals the process behind the organization of information; the initial note/ sketch for the card was photographed and reproduced on the reverse of the 'neat' side.

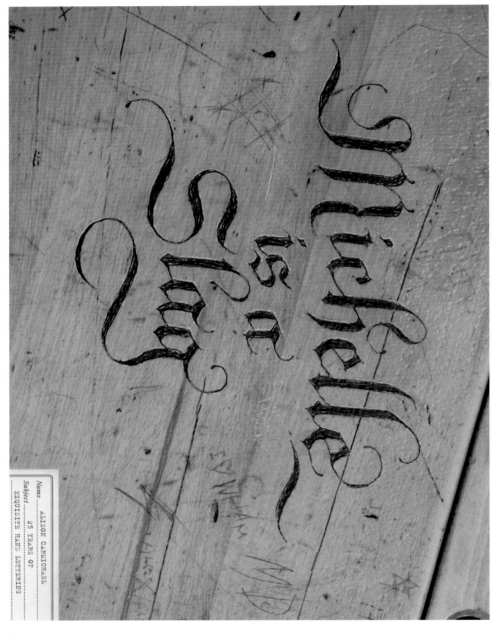

Design
Alison Carmichael

For
Alison Carmichael_
Hand-Lettering
Artist_
London, UK

Info
Combining hand-rendered type, litho printing and die-cutting, this facsimile of a traditional carte-de-visite format, realized using modern methods, perfectly approximates the crossover of old and new techniques that hand-lettering artist, Alison Carmichael, uses in her design practice.

Design
Sergio del Puerto_
Serial Cut™

For
Serial Cut™ _
Designer
Madrid, Spain

Info
A designer and image-maker who also specializes in drawn type, Sergio del Puerto is a digital wizard. His business card, though, revels in the tactile qualities of foil stamping and coated card stock, and features a cheeky "Call me".

Design
Blackbooks

For
Hi-Top Studio_
Boutique and
Recording Studio_
Fort Lauderdale,
USA

Info
Featuring hotrod-inspired custom lettering, die-cut and printed onto matboard, this business card marries street-style materials with an elegant, sinuous aesthetic.

Alex Cruz
954.305.3717
Charissa Schmitt
954.494.7492

Hi-Top Studio
700 SW 27th Ave
Ft Lauderdale, FL
954.703.6513

Design
Mark Smith_
Marksmith

For
Marksmith_
Designers_
London, UK

Info
Emphasizing their distinctive colour palette of pink and black, this card for Marksmith uses duplex black and pink card – sandwiched – along with matt foil for the contact details and gloss foil for the logo.

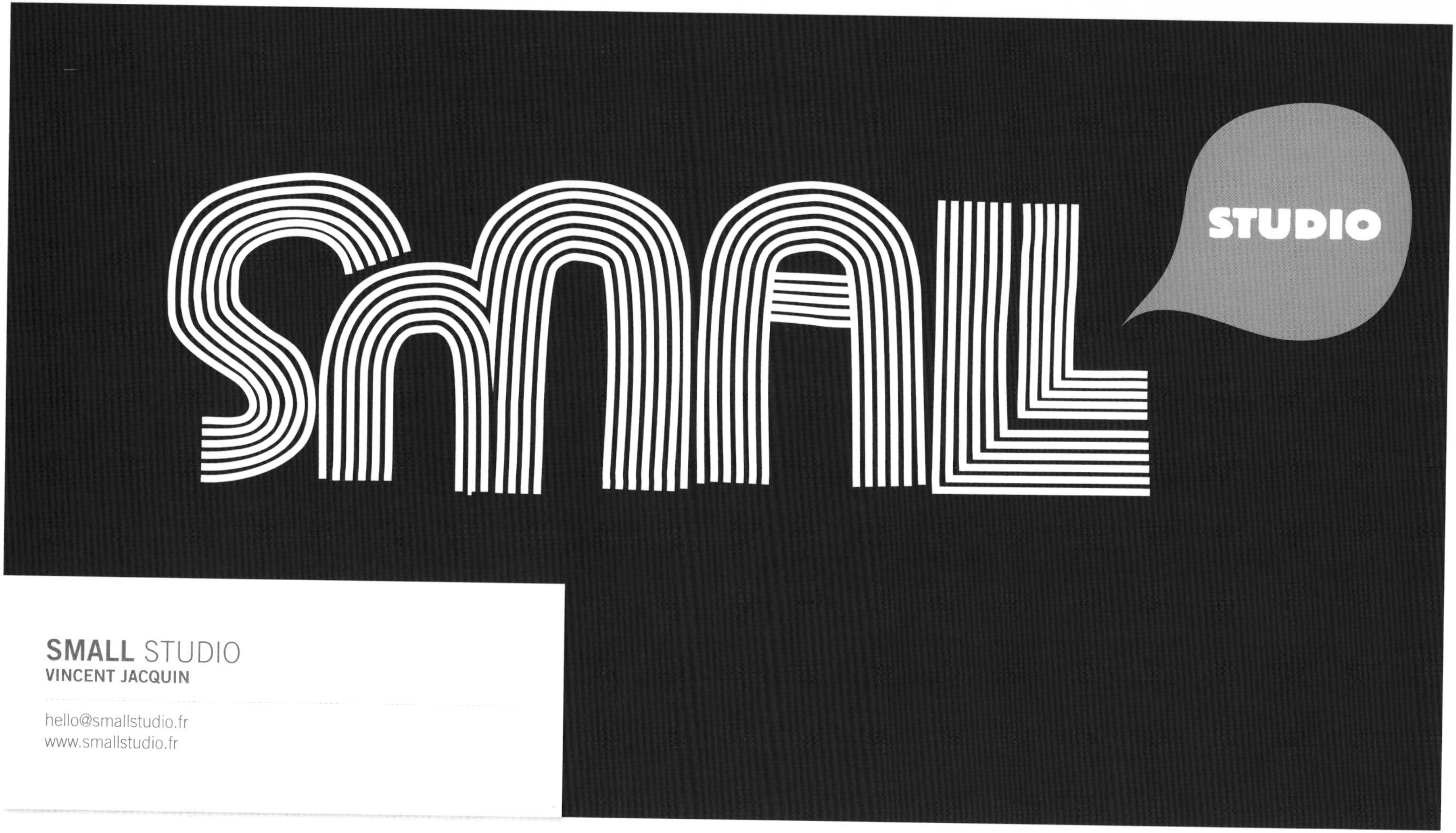

40

SMALL STUDIO
VINCENT JACQUIN

hello@smallstudio.fr
www.smallstudio.fr

Design
Vincent Jacquin_
Small Studio

For
Small Studio_
Designer,
Lyon, France

Info
Vincent Jacquin stretches the traditional business-card format
to incorporate various renditions of the Small Studio logo.

7pm—3am

**Freiburg Markthalle
Kaiser-Joseph-Strasse
79098 Freiburg
00 49 (0)761 7043 3155**

**The
Vegetable
Bar**

Design
David Azurdia_
Jamie Ellul_
Ben Christie_
Magpie Studio

For
The Vegetable Bar_
Café/Bar_
Freiburg, Germany

Info
Springing up each evening in a busy vegetable market as the stalls close down, this impromptu venue has become known to locals as The Vegetable Bar. Initially incorporating an upturned wine glass and a carrot, the identity grew to include other drink-and-vegetable combinations. The muted colour palette, for business cards and menus, reflects the earthy atmosphere and the subdued evening light inside the market building.

Design
12 Foot 6_
Darren Firth_
Alexandre Bettler_
Ben Casey_
Family_
David Bailey_

Clemens Baldermann_   Malcolm Garrett_
Corey Holms_   Matt Lambert_
Hideki Nakajima_   Pandarosa_
Billy Diaz_   Martin Shannon_
Carlos Segura_   Nicholas Felton_
Chris Lim_   Paul Davis_

For
Bunch,
Designers_
London, UK/
Zagreb, Croatia

Info
For Bunch's own rebrand they offered their logo to the design world, to be reinterpreted by the great and good. Invited designers were asked to "react" to the logo and sign their results. These "Bunchisms" were displayed on a website, and within months a whole lot more logos had been uploaded. The best have been applied to business cards, 127 at the last count, while each contributor gets a set of 32.

James Goggin_
Nicolas Ruston_
James Joyce_
David Quay_
Nicholas Felton

Gareth White_
Daniel Hägglund_
Ralph Burkhardt_
A.R.M._
Bruno Maag_

Damien Poulain_
François Chalet_
Ivo Sousa_
Jon Saunders_
Jonathan Ellery_

Apirat Infahsaeng_
M James_
Paul Insect_
Charles Lee_
Marcus Walters_

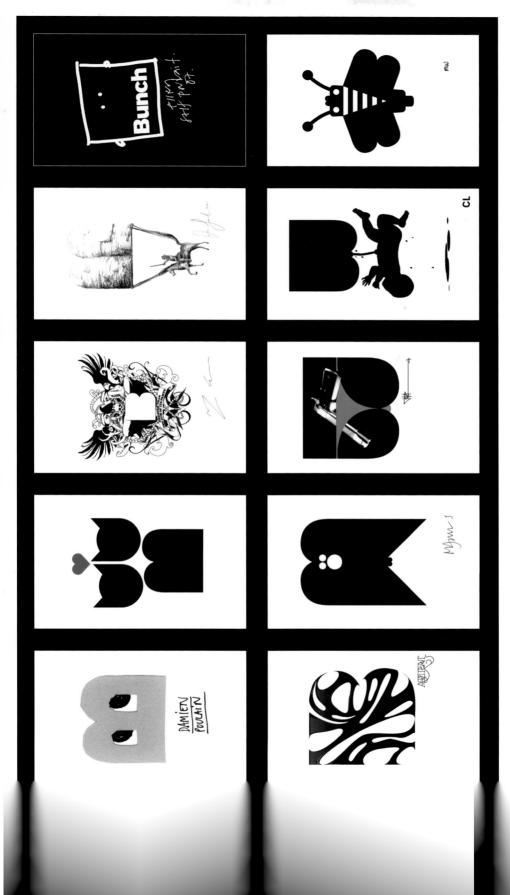

46

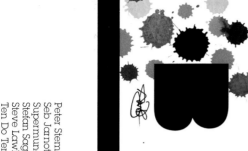

Peter Stemmler_
Seb Jarnot_
Supermundane_
Stefan Sagmeister_
Steve Lawler_
Ten Do Ten_

Alan Dye_
Aiden Grenelle_
Grandpeople_
Paul Willoughby_
Simon Whybray_
Nick Finney_

Lily Piyathaisere_
Chris Maibon_
OmegatheKidPhoenix_
John Downling_
Build_
Kelly Harland

Andrius Kirvela
+370 654 77991
andrius@petpunk.com
www.petpunk.com

Design
Andrius Kirvela_
Gediminas Šiaulys_
PetPunk

For
PetPunk_
Designers/Directors_
Vilnius, Lithuania

Info
Big, bold and in-your-face, featuring a bright green, spiky speech bubble (which positively screams) and a combination of cute and techno typography, this business card is over-sized, silk-screenprinted onto hefty board, and not intending to be forgotten.

Rosa de Jong | Creative
06 3070953
rosa@arcee.nl | www.arcee.nl

Clien Wintzen | Creative
06 5069621
clien@arcee.nl | www.arcee.nl

Bet your RC

Smart RC

Shake your RC

Kick some RC

Design
Rosa de Jong_
Clien Wintzen_
RC

For
RC_
Designers_
Amsterdam_
the Netherlands

Info
"We chose our name 'RC' because of our initials, but most of all because together they sound like arse: 'arsé.' Rather funny for a name that appears quite boring. And we'd like to 'kick some' by being different." De Jong and Wintzen also like to indulge their love of "handicraft" by hand-making each card, using stickers, stamps and textured card stock.

Mongrel Clothes & Accessories
050 5906419 – 050 3246768

Design
Chris Bolton

For
Mongrel_
Fashion Label_
Helsinki, Finland

Info
Expanding on elements from the fashion label's logo,
this business card creates a mini-world of Mongrel motifs.
The imagery is embossed, while the card stock is smooth
and coated.

Escalator
Import Disc & Cafe
Hotei Bldg, 3F -A,
2-31-3 Jinguame Shibuya-ku
Tokyo 150-0001 / Japan
Tel +81 (0)3 5775 13 15
shop@escalator.co.jp
www.escalator.co.jp

<u>Info</u>
Uncoated stock and black-and-white printing, not to mention
a wobbly skull logo, cut-up photos and hand-lettering, add up
to a DIY punk aesthetic that perfectly describes the taste and
ambience of this alternative establishment.

<u>Design</u>
Chris Bolton

<u>For</u>
Escalator Records_
Record Label/
Import Record
Shop/Café_
Tokyo, Japan

MARC ATKINSON

MARC&ANNA
Studio 46
Regent Studios
8 Andrews Road
London E8 4QN

T 020 7249 6111
M 07766 657 142
E marc@marcandanna.co.uk
www.marcandanna.co.uk

ANNA EKELUND

MARC&ANNA
Studio 46
Regent Studios
8 Andrews Road
London E8 4QN

T 020 7249 6111
M 07766 202 087
E anna@marcandanna.co.uk
www.marcandanna.co.uk

CONNIE WRIGHT

MARC&ANNA
Studio 46
Regent Studios
8 Andrews Road
London E8 4QN

T 020 7249 6111
E connie@marcandanna.co.uk
www.marcandanna.co.uk

HELLO!

MARC&ANNA
Studio 46
Regent Studios
8 Andrews Road
London E8 4QN

T 020 7249 6111
E hello@marcandanna.co.uk
www.marcandanna.co.uk

Design
Marc Atkinson_
Anna Ekelund_
Marc & Anna

For
Marc & Anna_
Designers
London, UK

Info
A series of business cards shows off a collection of "found" ampersands in a wide range of graphic styles, both historical and contemporary. The ampersands are hand-stamped additions to pre-printed cards. This customized element points up the personality – and attention to detail – that this young design company offer.

HELLO!

MARC & ANNA
Studio 46
Regent Studios
8 Andrews Road
London E8 4QN

T 020 7249 6111
E hello@marcandanna.co.uk
www.marcandanna.co.uk

HELLO!

MARC & ANNA
Studio 46
Regent Studios
8 Andrews Road
London E8 4QN

T 020 7249 6111
E hello@marcandanna.co.uk
www.marcandanna.co.uk

HELLO!

MARC & ANNA
Studio 46
Regent Studios
8 Andrews Road
London E8 4QN

T 020 7249 6111
E hello@marcandanna.co.uk
www.marcandanna.co.uk

CONNIE WRIGHT

MARC & ANNA
Studio 46
Regent Studios
8 Andrews Road
London E8 4QN

T 020 7249 6111
E connie@marcandanna.co.uk
www.marcandanna.co.uk

הצופה

להזמנות: 03-5690447
הכתובת: רחוב הסבר 66
הדואר: HATZOFE.CO.il

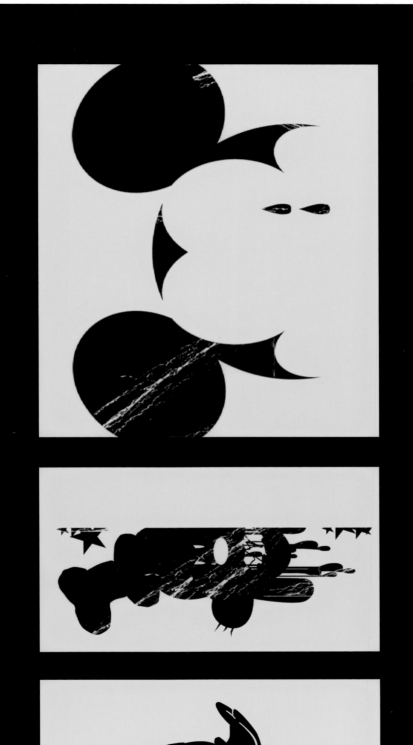

Design
Shin Yaron_
Jewboy Corp™

For
Hatzofe Club_
Tel Aviv, Israel

Info
Using Pantone black and yellow on recycled card stock, this set of eye-catching business cards reproduces elements from iconic cartoon characters as mysterious silhouettes – combined with various graphic embellishments – to create streetwise versions of childhood favourites.

Design
Clemens
Baldermann_
Purple Haze Studio

For
Purple Haze Studio_
Designer/
Art Director_
Munich, Germany

Info
Featuring a virtuoso logotype – reminiscent of the golden era of album cover graphics and the sort of band logos that were scratched into the tops of school desks – Purple Haze designer Clemens Baldermann cleverly 'bags' the glossy black business card to protect its perfection.

CLEMENS BALDERMANN
GRAPHIC DESIGN & ART DIRECTION

MOBILE: +49 (0)1 72-6 68 85 83
MAIL: CLEMENS@THEPURPLEHAZE.NET
WEB: WWW.THEPURPLEHAZE.NET

Design
Julien Crouïgneau_
Design June

For
VU_
Merchandising/
Brand Consultants_
France

Info
Using two colours and a UV varnish, Design June create a high-touch, super-slick business card that radiates sophistication and showcases a powerful 3D logotype.

Design
Matt Willey_
Studio8 Design

For
Plastique Publishing_
Magazine Publisher_
London, UK

Info
Described as a luxurious, high-end fashion magazine, Plastique needed a business card that signalled glamour, quality and independence. The logo is realized using clear foil blocking, while the contact details appear on the reverse in purple foil. The fashion connection is underlined by the heavyweight card stock, which is more often used for expensive shoeboxes.

Kate Zindht
Assistant Sportswear Editor
Plastique, 93 Shepperton Road
Top Floor, London, UK, N1 3DF
Mobile +44 (0)771 967 2107
Kate2000@yahoo.com

BLEACH

Design
Shin Yaron_
Jewboy Corp™

For
Bleach Clothing_
Tel Aviv, Israel

Info
A no-nonsense logo is printed white out of black on recycled stock; with the addition of an accidental stain, it's as if this design was achieved using bleach itself.

Design
Shin Yaron_
Jewboy Corp™

For
Hood Clothing_
Tel Aviv, Israel

Info
Using friends as models and artists as designers, this limited-edition clothing line presents custom-made garments featuring found images, distressed surfaces and graphic devices. A series of posters, postcards and business cards is used to promote the line.

Design
Jernej Stritar_
Urh Sobočan_
Tricikel

For
Tricikel_
Designers /
Illustrators_
Ljubljana, Slovenia

Info
This double-sided business card features contact details in two languages and presents the logo as a playful collection of letters and numbers, flipped and reversed.

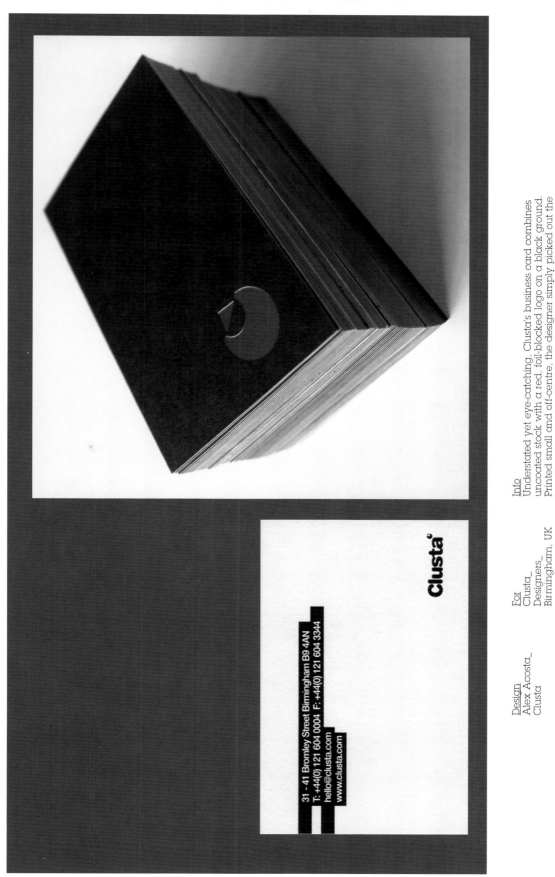

Info
Understated yet eye-catching, Clusta's business card combines
uncoated stock with a red, foil-blocked logo on a black ground.
Printed small and off-centre, the designer simply picked out the
logo in colour and resisted the urge to overuse the foil.

For
Clusta_
Designers_
Birmingham, UK

Design
Alex Acosta_
Clusta

31 - 41 Bromley Street Birmingham B9 4AN
T: +44(0) 121 604 0004 F: +44(0) 121 604 3344
hello@clusta.com
www.clusta.com

Clusta

<u>Design</u>
Airside

<u>For</u>
Airside_
Designers/
Illustrators/
Animators_
London, UK

<u>Info</u>
To celebrate their tenth anniversary, Airside created a new identity, including this set of business cards, which features abstracted silhouette portraits of all staff members. This "grown-up" aesthetic cleverly hints at Airside's expertise in the fields of moving image, illustration and animation, without foregrounding any one particular style.

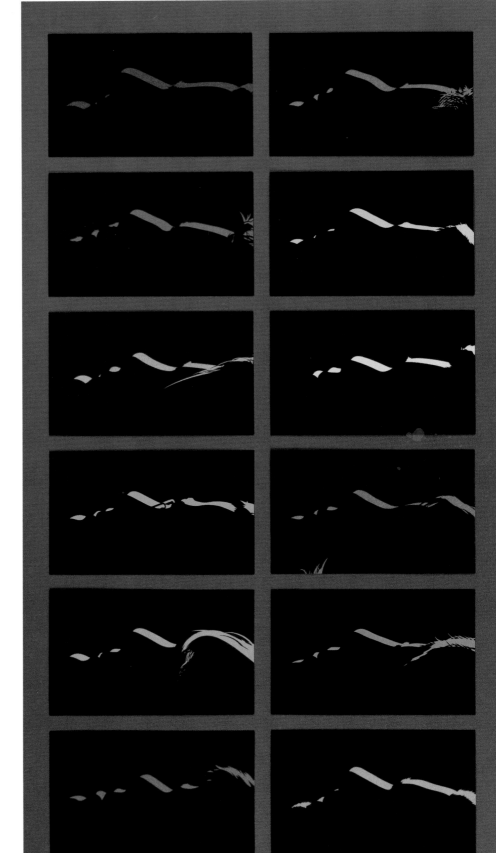

Airside Airside
Airside Airside
Airside Airside

Standard 8

Standard 8 Ltd
2 Station Street, Lewes
East Sussex BN7 2DA
United Kingdom

T +44 (0)1273 488 330
F +44 (0)1273 488 774
www.standardeight.com

Design_
Nick Jones_
Stephen McGilvray_
Browns

For
Standard 8_
Design and
Manufacture_
London, UK

Info
To reflect the fact that Standard 8 is anything but standard –
designing everything from one-off pieces of furniture to exhibition
systems – this set of business cards features eight different logos,
each made of 'figures of eight', and using various typefaces.
The resultant flower-like symbols, or fleurons, are brought to life
in fluorescent foil.

72

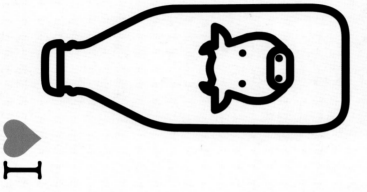

I ♥
natashashah.co.uk
+44.(0)7980.719.553

I ♥
natashashah.co.uk
+44.(0)7980.719.553

Design
Natasha Shah_
Design Friendship

For
Natasha Shah_
Designer_
London, UK

Info
Young graphic designer Natasha Shah helped her local corner shop maximize its visibility by designing a giant mural featuring products as icons. She borrowed these for her set of "I Heart NY"-inspired business cards.

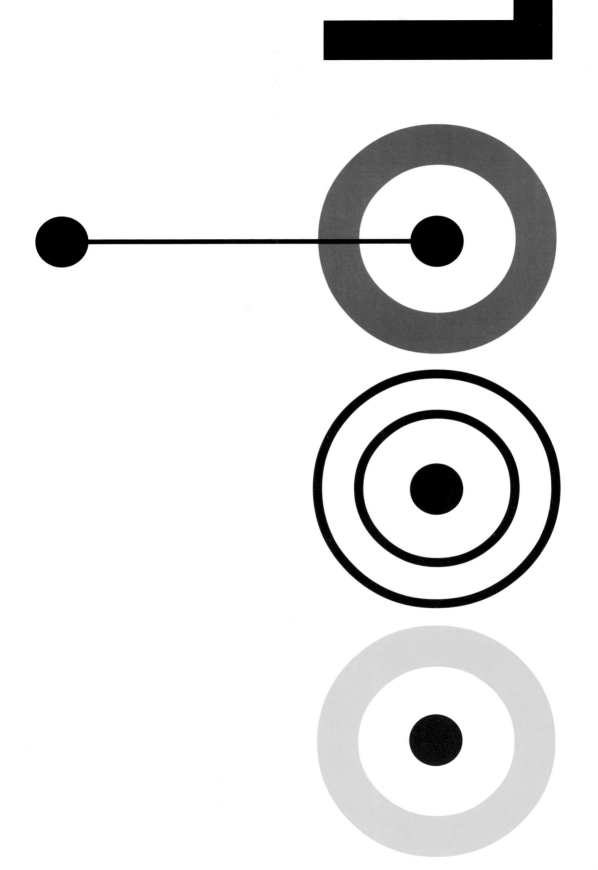

VOLT

• animation

VOLT

• film production

VOLT

• post production
• film production
• audio
• animation

Eda Arikan

1. Levent Mahallesi
Çalıkusu Sokak No:14
34330 Besiktas Istanbul

T: +90 212 283 10 01
F: +90 212 283 10 03

eda.arikan@1000volt.com.tr
www.1000volt.com.tr

Design
Bianca Wendt

For
1000 Volt_
Film/Animation/
Post-Production
Company_
Istanbul, Turkey

Info
Bianca Wendt has developed a flexible identity for this multi-tasking company to reflect four distinct but related areas of expertise, using abstractions of DVD, television, video and audio cables. The business cards are personalized to indicate each staff member's speciality.

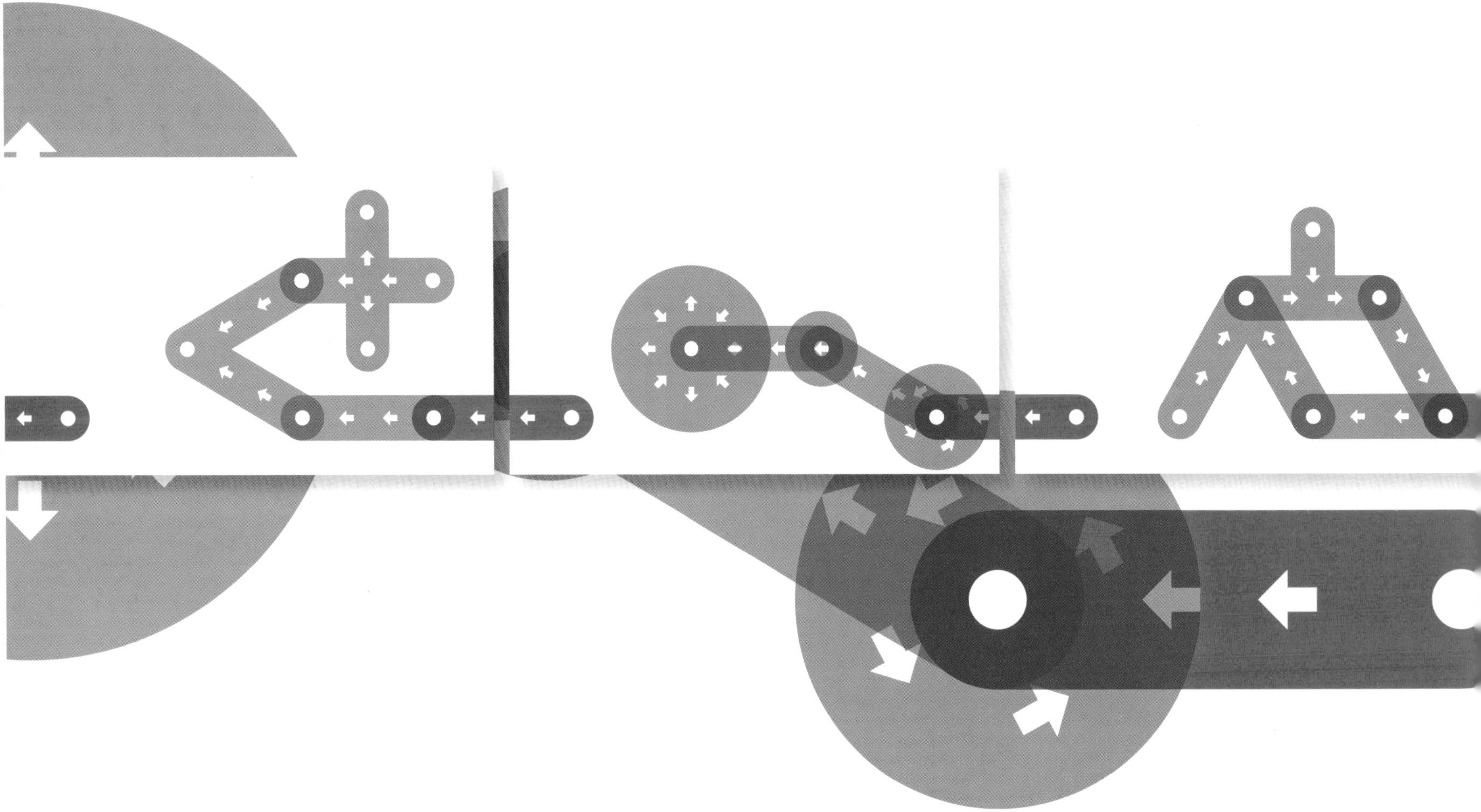

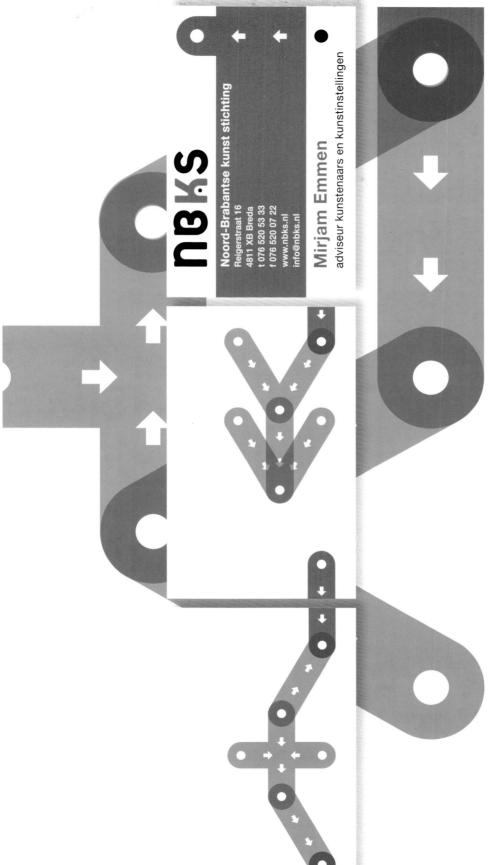

nBKS

Noord-Brabantse kunst stichting

Reigerstraat 16
4811 XB Breda
t 076 520 53 33
f 076 520 07 22
www.nbks.nl
info@nbks.nl

Mirjam Emmen
adviseur kunstenaars en kunstinstellingen

Design
Richard Pijs_
Fourpack
Ontwerpers

For
NBKS_
Professional Artists'
Centre_
Breda,
the Netherlands

Info
This series of business cards, featuring a continuous illustration
reminiscent of construction toys such as Meccano, emphasizes
the connectivity and flow of information at NBKS, which offers
advice, workshops and gallery space to practising artists.

FINE™

HTTP
: //
WWW.DESIGNIS-FINE.COM | DESIGNISFINE@GMAIL.COM | 720 635 0106
CELESTE PREVOST ENJOYS GRAPHIC DESIGN

Design
Celeste Prevost_
Designisfine™

For
Designisfine™ _
Designer,
Minneapolis, USA

Info
As part of a whole host of self-promotional projects, Celeste Prevost developed a pink-and-black skull-and-critters identity, here shown on her business card. Other applications include sets of button badges, stickers and a zine.

Design
Adrienne Bornstein_
Pierre Sponchiado_
Bornstein &
Sponchiado

For
Zotoprod_
Art-Buying Agency_
Paris, France

Info
A monogram-like Z, complete with an extra flourish and realized in gold ink on a heavy, velvety card stock, adds up to a sophisticated, chic identity and a business card with gravitas.

ZOTOPROD

Design
Alex Acosta_
Clusta

For
Claudia Mahecha
Design_
Interior Designer
San Francisco, USA

Info
This contemporary interior designer's boldly sophisticated yet
feminine logo is translated into a business card using foil blocking
on a black card stock.

Design
Sarah Boris

For
The Royal
Philharmonic
Society_
Creative
Benefactors_
London, UK

Info
Sarah Boris created a decorative illustration incorporating musical notation to be used across all the stationery for this music-focused charity. Despite budgetary restrictions, the business card is an elegant attention-seeker. © The Royal Philharmonic Society.

The Royal
Philharmonic
Society

10 Stratford Place London W1C 1BA
Phone +44 (0)20 7491 8110
Fax +44 (0)20 7493 7463
Email admin@royalphilharmonicsociety.org.uk
www.royalphilharmonicsociety.org.uk

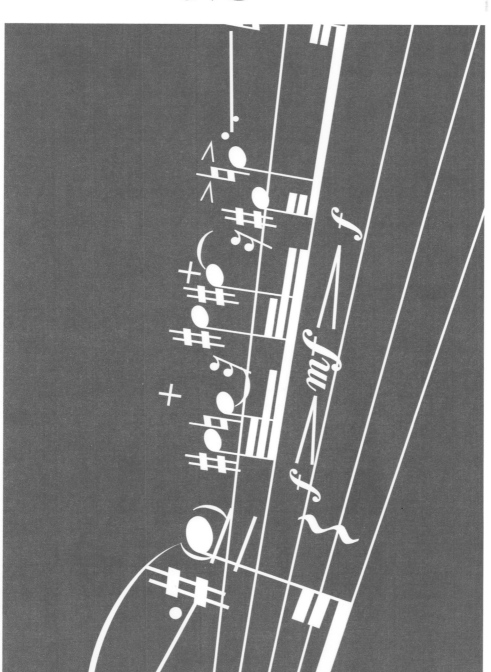

Design_
Johannes Grummond_
Tom Mesquitta

For_
String Films_
Film Production
Company_
London, UK

Info_
For this production company specializing in films about green
issues, the designers combined a ball of string and a film reel
to create a dynamic logo and business card. Nothing could be
simpler than using string, but 'How long is a piece of string?' is an
age-old conundrum, and here it sums up perfectly the complexity
and simplicity of this company's approach.

Ben Gray
Producer

M: 07973 430905
T: 020 8944 6874
ben@stringfilms.com
www.stringfilms.com

StringFilms

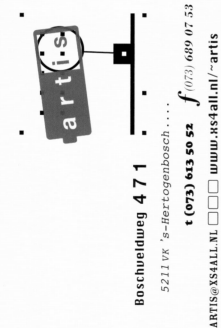

Boschveldweg 4 7 1

5211 VK 's-Hertogenbosch....

t (073) 613 50 52   *f (073) 689 07 53*

ARTIS@XS4ALL.NL □□□ **www.xs4all.nl/~artis**

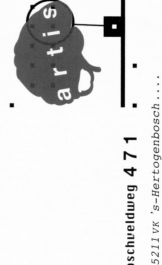

Boschveldweg 4 7 1

5211 VK 's-Hertogenbosch....

t (073) 613 50 52   *f (073) 689 07 53*

ARTIS@XS4ALL.NL □□□ **www.xs4all.nl/~artis**

Boschveldweg 4 7 1

5211 VK 's-Hertogenbosch....

t (073) 613 50 52   *f (073) 689 07 53*

ARTIS@XS4ALL.NL □□□ **www.xs4all.nl/~artis**

Boschveldweg 4 7 1

5211 VK 's-Hertogenbosch....

t (073) 613 50 52   *f (073) 689 07 53*

ARTIS@XS4ALL.NL □□□ **www.xs4all.nl/~artis**

Info
Printed one colour with black ink, a single design is transformed into a series of business cards by the addition of various rubber-stamped images in a range of colours: the ambiguous symbols, some man-made, some natural, are positioned as part of the organization's logo, turning an information-laden card into a more whimsical statement.

For
Artis_
Professional
Artists' Centre_
's-Hertogenbosch,
the Netherlands

Design
Richard Pijs_
Fourpack Ontwerpers

Design
Start Creative

For
Breed,
Illustration Agency_
London, UK

Info
From a precise grid of points, a logotype organically emerges to reveal a new kind of illustration agency. Small but perfectly formed, this "boutique" agency represents a coterie of specially chosen artists, and negotiates with the world's biggest brands.

Olivia Triggs Director

Breed Limited
Medius House
First Floor, 2 Sheraton Street
Soho, London W1F 8BH

tel. +44 (0) 207 269 0196
mob. +44 (0) 7775 992 006
em. olivia@breedlondon.com
web. www.breedlondon.com

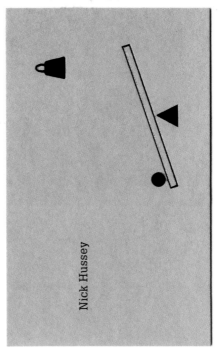

Touchpoint.

206 Falcon Works
Copperfield Road
London E3 4RT

david@touchpointcontracts.com
www.touchpointcontracts.com

07976 258993

Nick Hussey

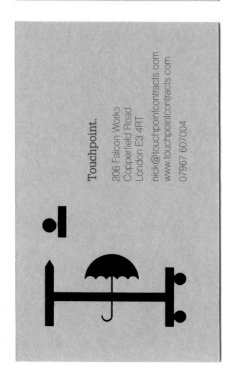

Touchpoint.

206 Falcon Works
Copperfield Road
London E3 4RT

nick@touchpointcontracts.com
www.touchpointcontracts.com

07967 607004

Touchpoint.

206 Falcon Works
Copperfield Road
London E3 4RT

olivia@touchpointcontracts.com
www.touchpointcontracts.com

07730 979509

Info
For this company that "makes stuff happen", HarrimanSteel designed a fluid, process-led logo, featuring various starting points, catalysts and unknowable outcomes. The combination of tactile, grey card stock and black embossing creates a simple schematic, with a hint of the surreal.

For
Touch Point_
Creative Team
Project Managers_
London, UK

Design
George Wu
Creative Direction
Julian Dickinson_
Nick Steel_
HarrimanSteel

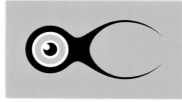

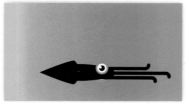

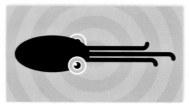

Info
Twelve different squid mascots were created for a roving gang of international account planners, and were applied to a series of 48 cards, giving each individual a choice of squid!

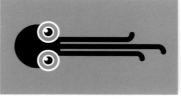

London, UK/
New York, USA

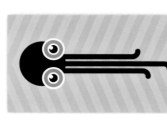

For
Open Intelligence
Agency_
Account Planners_
Sydney, Australia/
Amsterdam,
the Netherlands/

Design
Stefan G. Bucher_
344 Design, LLC

Refreshing!

BLINK PRODUCTIONS LTD.

181 Wardour St, London W1F 8WZ. *www.blinkprods.com*

Tel +44 20 7494 0747 ★ Fax +44 20 7494 3771

✻ e:info@blinkprods.com ... Yum, Yum!

Design
Mark Denton_
Mark Denton
Design

Typography
Andy Dymock

For
Blink Productions_
Advertising
Film Production
Company_
London, UK

Info
Created for a production company with a roster of rule-breaking directors, these business cards aim to replicate the diversity of talent on offer. The wood-effect cards are customized with a "logo" from a range of stickers featuring spoof vintage product packaging (for soap powder, choccie biscuits, pet food).

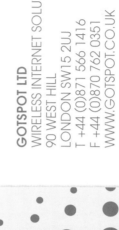

GOTSPOT LTD
WIRELESS INTERNET SOLUTIONS
90 WEST HILL
LONDON SW15 2UJ
T +44 (0)871 566 1416
F +44 (0)870 762 0351
WWW.GOTSPOT.CO.UK

TIM BOWER
DIRECTOR
M +44 (0)7966 014212
TIM@GOTSPOT.CO.UK

Info
Various two-colour dot and spiral designs are used on this set of
business cards to represent a 'central hot spot' from which the
wireless Internet service emanates. The palette of teal blue and
scarlet red on snowy-white stock is playfully retro-futuristic.

For
Gotspot_
Wireless Internet
Consultants_
London, UK

Design
Fivefootsix

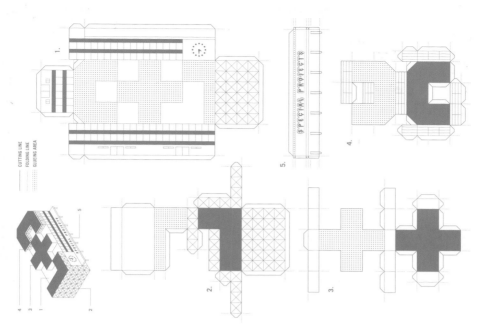

CUTTING LINE
FOLDING LINE
GLUEING AREA

1.

SPECIAL PROJECTS

5.

4.

2.

3.

Design
Natasha Shah_
Chris Hilton_
Design Friendship

For
Lee & Dan Special
Projects_
Directors_
London, UK

Info
Responding to a brief to reflect the humorous, bold and experimental nature of these tongue-in-cheeky directors, the identity quickly grew into a "house of cards" research establishment and headquarters building for loyal fans to construct. As the brand colours are fluorescent, the business cards are screenprinted with a double hit of colour.

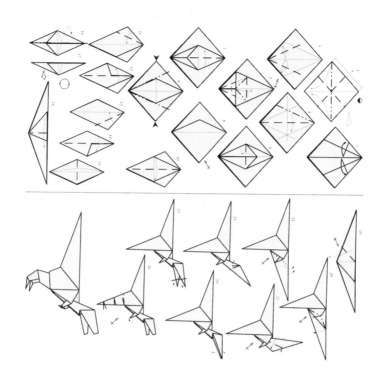

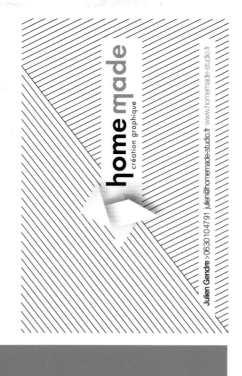

Julien Gendre >0630104791 julien@homemade-studio.fr www.homemade-studio.fr

Design
Julien Gendre_
Home Made Studio

For
Home Made Studio_
Designer_
Lyon, France

Info
This series of business cards and postcards presents a playful identity for, in Julien Gendre's own words, "a home-alone, self-made graphic designer".

WWW.MORTENLAURSEN.COM   INFO@MORTENLAURSEN.COM

Design
Morten Laursen_
Ulla Puggaard

For
Morten Laursen_
Photographer_
London, UK

Info
Fashion and beauty photographer Morten Laursen is at home shooting glamorous women and groovy gadgets, and mixing editorial and advertising commissions. His business cards, co-designed with Ulla Puggaard, feature a distinctive "crest" and a series of his most experimental images.

Design
Daniel Westwood_
Family

For
Family_
Designer_
Birmingham, UK

Info
A lover of stripes and blobby typefaces, Daniel Westwood
has created a business card with a show-stopping vibrancy,
achieved with the simplest of means: black ink on white stock.

TIME BASED™

Timebased Events

G10 Union Wharf
23–25 Wenlock Road
London N1 7SB

T (44) 020 7608 0080
F (44) 020 7608 0081
M (44) 07970 186 290
richard@timebased.co.uk
www.timebased.co.uk

Richard Dodgson
Creative Director

Design
Steve Payne_
Studio Output

For
Timebased_
Events Company_
London, UK

Info
An illustrated world of time-based happenings, from flowers blooming to clocks ticking, is contrasted with the bold wrap-around logo, which incorporates minute and second symbols.

Design
Mark Smith_
Rus Mann_
Marksmith

For
Attention Seekers_
Brand
Entertainment_
London, UK

Info
With an identity based on three-dimensional arrows intersecting at dynamic angles, this black-on-white business card underlines the fast-forward appeal of a multimedia consultancy.

Ben Bailey

+ 44 (0) 7957 489055
ben@attentionseekers.tv

69 Gloucester Avenue
Primrose Hill
London NW1 8LD

+ 44 (0) 20 7209 5966
www.attentionseekers.tv

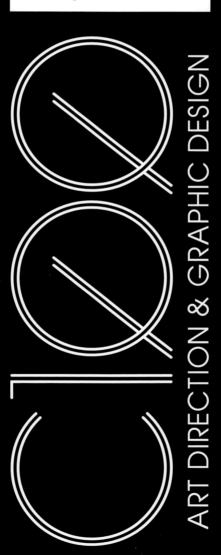

CHRISTIAN HUNDERTMARK

C100
SCHWEIGERSTR. 8
81541 MÜNCHEN
GERMANY

T/F +49.89.65309520
M +49.177.3668528
HELLO@C100STUDIO.COM
WWW.C100STUDIO.COM

ART DIRECTION & GRAPHIC DESIGN

Design
Christian
Hundertmark_
C100 Studio

For
C100 Studio_
Designers_
Munich, Germany

Info
This one-colour business card, with a hot foil stamp, gives a
no-nonsense look – timeless and informative – to a young studio
that specializes in media, entertainment, fashion and culture.

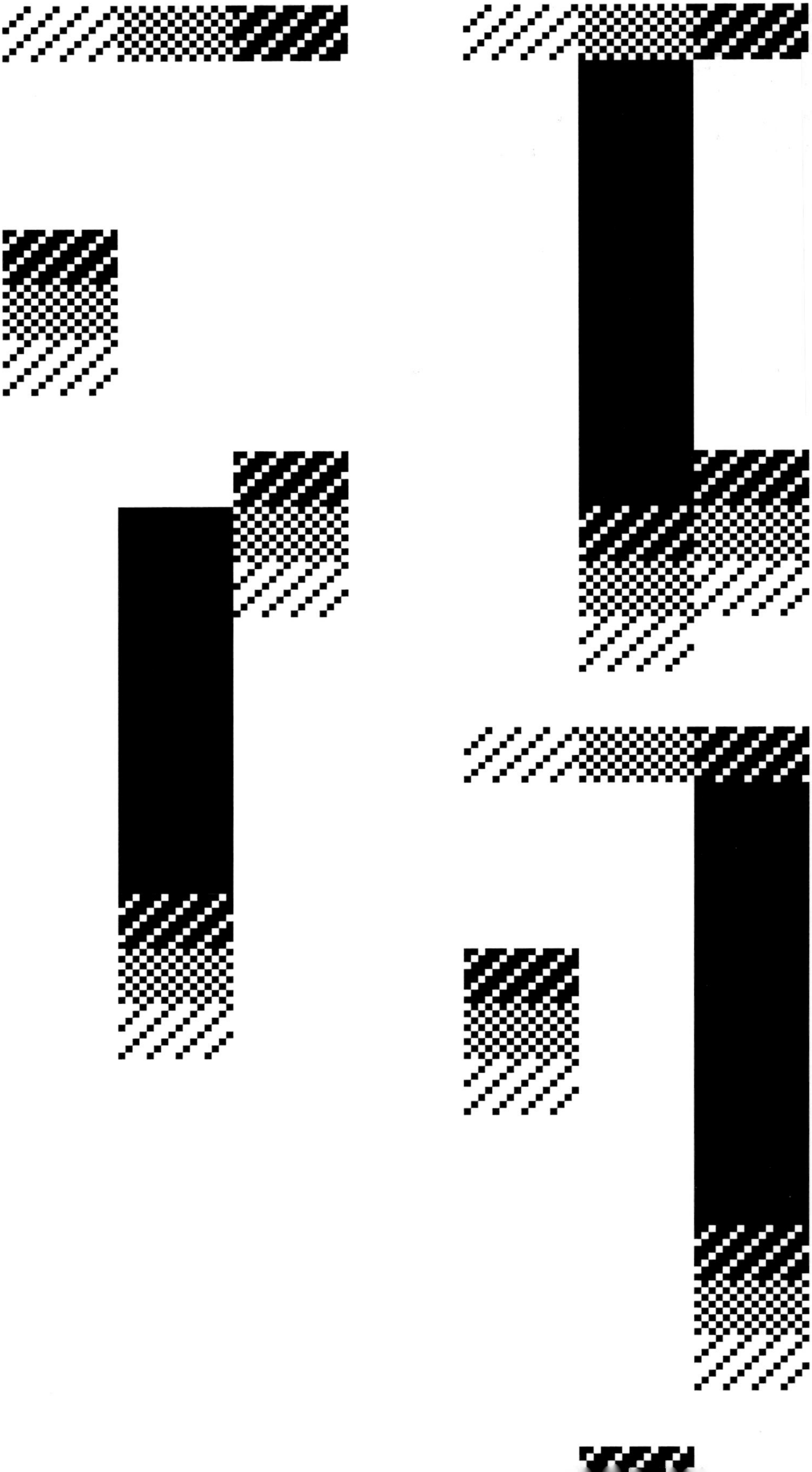

Design
Coolmix

For
Coolmix_
Designers_
Berlin, Germany

Info
Experts in image-overload, Coolmix create eye-popping graphics for moving-image and print projects. Mixing pixel patterns and bitmap type, these business cards speak the studio's own aesthetic language.

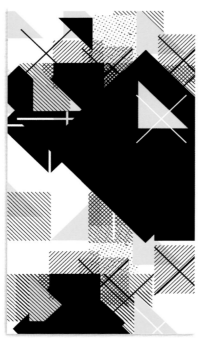

ALPHABET SOUP

Michael Vati
info@alphabet-soup.com.au

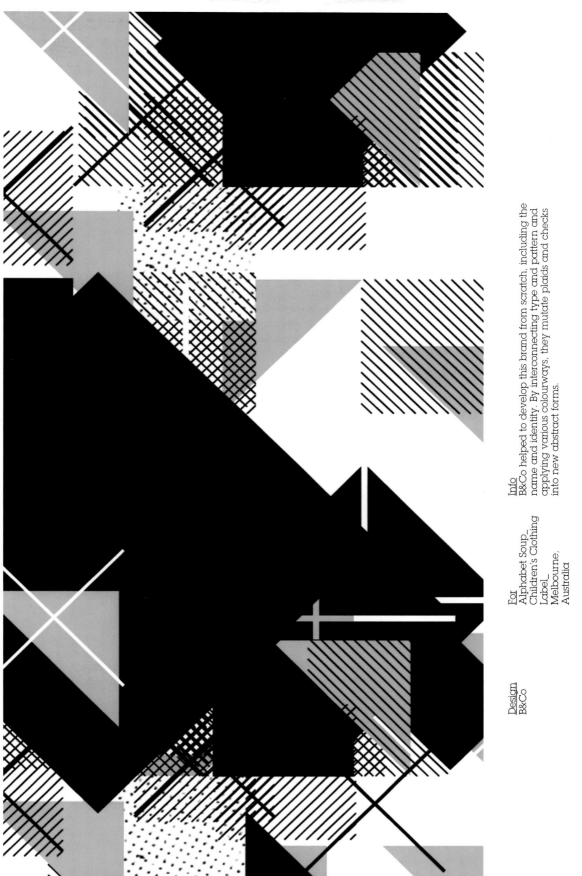

Info
B&Co helped to develop this brand from scratch, including the name and identity. By interconnecting type and pattern and applying various colourways, they mutate plaids and checks into new abstract forms.

For
Alphabet Soup_
Children's Clothing
Label_
Melbourne,
Australia

Design
B&Co

Brendan Elliott
Creative Director

brendan@bnco.com.au
bnco.com.au

Terry Ricardo
Designer

terry@bnco.com.au
bnco.com.au

Design
B&Co

For
B&Co_
Designers_
Melbourne,
Australia

Info
To demonstrate the versatility of this youth-oriented design studio,
dynamic cut-up collages, mixing pattern, mark-making and
ambiguous silhouettes, are backed by a reverse side that is cool
and understated, with a hint of humour.

bnco.com.au

B&Co

$pend some time...
make some $...

with

B&Co

B&Co

MIKE CARNEY
IMAGE MAKER / DESIGNER
+44 (0)151 414 3325 / 07773 197 111
MIKE@MIKESSTUDIO.co.uk

MIKE'S STUDIO

WWW.MIKESSTUDIO.CO.UK
ON THE ARCHIVE OF
COMMISSIONED PROJECTS
ILLUSTRATION & PHOTOGRAPHY
BEATS / GROOVES / VIBES
IDEAS & STUFF

Mike's Studio

Mike's Studio

MIKE CARNEY
IMAGE MAKER / DESIGNER
+44 (0)151 414 3325 / 07773 197 111
MIKE@MIKESSTUDIO.co.uk

MIKE CARNEY
IMAGE MAKER / DESIGNER
+44 (0)151 414 3325 / 07773 197 111
MIKE@MIKESSTUDIO.co.uk

MIKE'S STUDIO

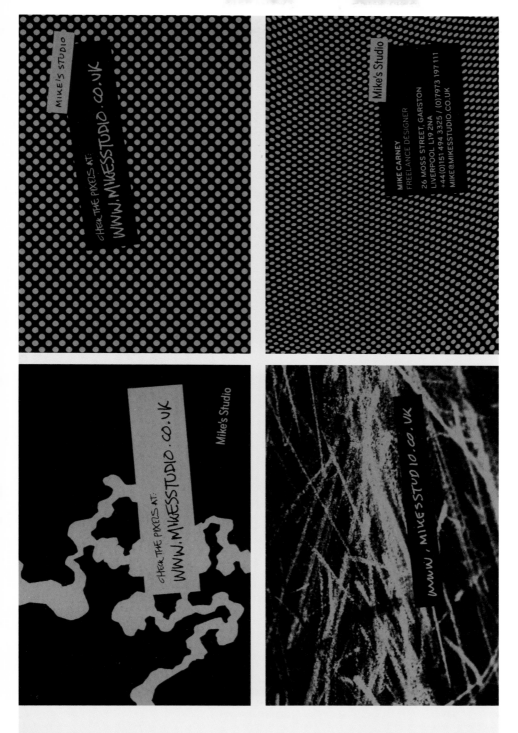

Mike's Studio

CHECK THE PIXELS AT:
WWW.MIKESSTUDIO.CO.UK

MIKE'S STUDIO

MIKE CARNEY
FREELANCE DESIGNER

26 MOSS STREET, GARSTON
LIVERPOOL L19 2NA
+44(0)151 494 3325 / (0)7973 197 111
MIKE@MIKESSTUDIO.CO.UK

WWW.MIKESSTUDIO.CO.UK

Design
Mike Carney_
Mike's Studio

For
Mike's Studio_
Designer_
Liverpool, UK

Info
Combining hand-lettering, eye-popping patterns, energetic mark-making and a cut-and-paste aesthetic – employing black ink on fluorescent card stock – Mike Carney's business cards both engage and entertain.

ROBERT MORISSEY
DIRECTION DIRECTOR
robert.morissey@nurun.com
nurun.com

nurun
DIGITAL STRATEGIES ®

75 FIFTH STREET NW
SUITE 600
ATLANTA GA 30308 - USA

TEL 404 876-7226
FAX 404 591-1650

Design
Julien Crouigneau_
Design June

For
Nurun_
Interactive
Communications
Agency_
Atlanta, USA

Info
This shaped business card echoes the shifted geometry of
Nurun's logotype, while the multiple icons represent the
different countries in which this global company operates
and finds inspiration.

114

Design
Sara Oakley_
Studio Output

For
Annie Greenabelle_
Fashion Label,
Nottingham, UK

Info
This fashion label uses organic and recycled fabrics, but steers away from the "worthy" look by employing contemporary yet feminine colours and patterns. The business cards are printed on recycled card stock, and double as swing tags with the addition of a die-cut hole.

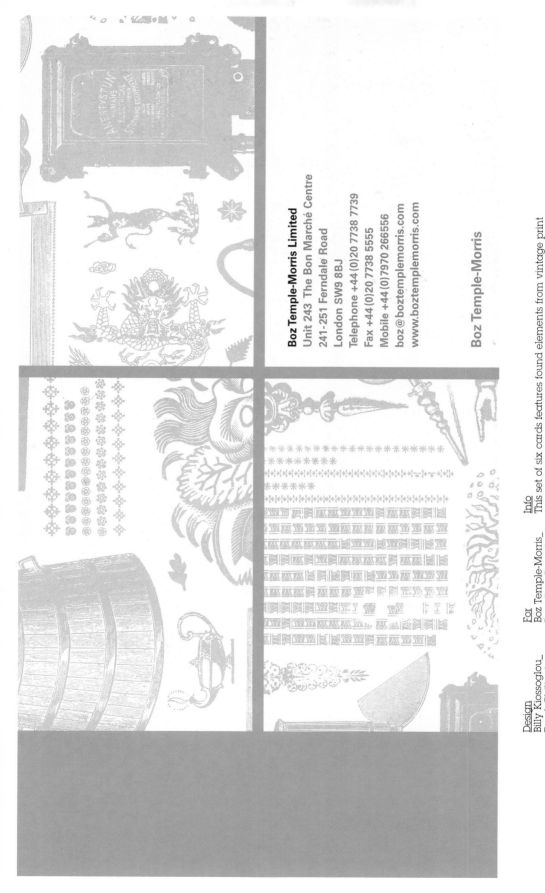

Boz Temple-Morris Limited
Unit 243 The Bon Marché Centre
241-251 Ferndale Road
London SW9 8BJ
Telephone +44 (0)20 7738 7739
Fax +44 (0)20 7738 5555
Mobile +44 (0)7970 266556
boz@boztemplemorris.com
www.boztemplemorris.com

Boz Temple-Morris

Design
Billy Kiossoglou_
Frank Philippin_
Brighten the Corners

For
Boz Temple-Morris
Branding Consultant_
London, UK

Info
This set of six cards features found elements from vintage print jobs and letterpress archives. The diverse imagery underlines this consultant's versatility in working across commercial and artistic projects.

DEUCE creative

megan mcbride communications director
megan@deucecreative.com

1518 washington
suite g
houston, tx 77007
o 713 863 8633
f 713 863 8647
m 832 326 9163

Art of Strategy
deucecreative.com

DEUCE creative

jenny nicholas designer
jenny@deucecreative.com

1518 washington
suite g
houston, tx 77007
o 713 863 8633
f 713 863 8647
m 817 437 0906

Art of Strategy
deucecreative.com

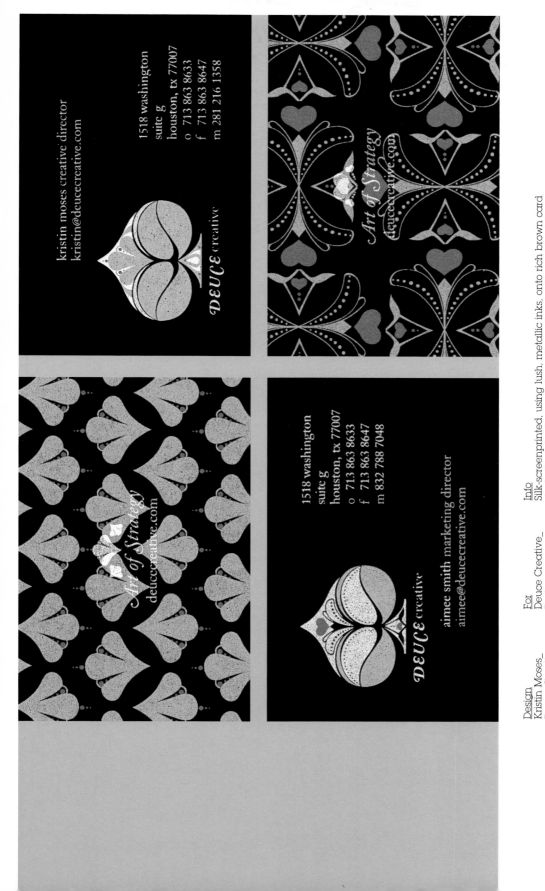

kristin moses creative director
kristin@deucecreative.com

1518 washington
suite g
houston, tx 77007
o 713 863 8633
f 713 863 8647
m 281 216 1358

DEUCE creative

Art of Strategy
deucecreative.com

Art of Strategy
deucecreative.com

1518 washington
suite g
houston, tx 77007
o 713 863 8633
f 713 863 8647
m 832 788 7048

aimee smith marketing director
aimee@deucecreative.com

DEUCE creative

Design
Kristin Moses_
Deuce Creative

For
Deuce Creative_
Designers_
Houston, USA

Info
Silk-screenprinted, using lush, metallic inks, onto rich brown card
stock, these business cards are decorative, tactile and feminine.
The set allows each staff member to combine a personal pattern
and colour palette.

Generate / Commotion

Design
Steve Jocktisch

Writer
Joel Stacy

Creative Direction
William Jurewicz_
Riley Kane_
Jason Strong_
Space150

For
Space150_
Designers_
Los Angeles/
Minneapolis/
New York, USA

Info
"We are over-committed to evolution," explain Space150, which is why they change their identity every 150 days. The Generate Change set of business cards (known as version 10.8) represents the generation of inspiration, and retains a simple-yet-sophisticated, cool-yet-futuristic aesthetic.

Generate / **Goodness**

Generate / **Goosebumps**

Generate / **Revelry**

Generation X8

space150

William J. Jurewicz
Chief Executive Officer
wjj@space150.com

Direct 612 460 2803

space150.com

Minneapolis | Los Angeles | New York

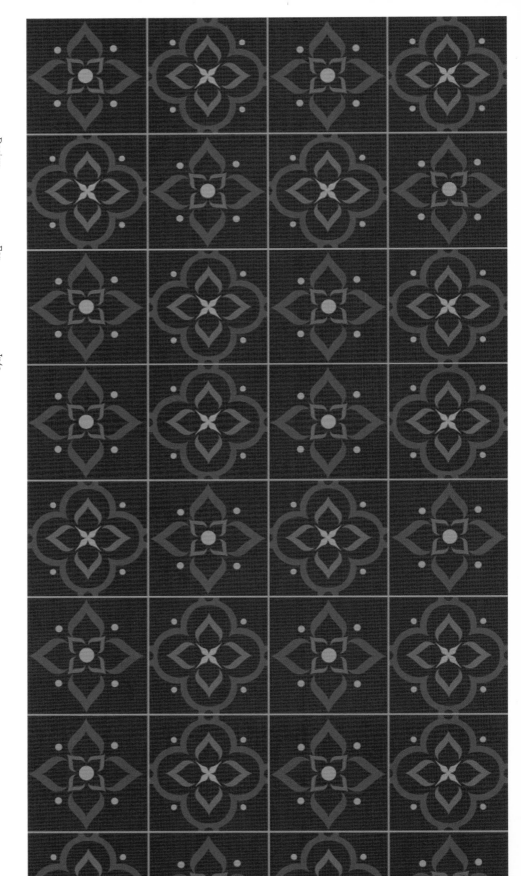

Design
Erika Kim_
Studio Chavéz

For
Studio Chavéz_
Designer,
Los Angeles, USA

Info
To showcase her knowledge of the Hispanic community in the USA, Erika Kim combines a pattern inspired by traditional Mexican design, with a logo based on the Aztec calendar, to produce this high-profile business card.

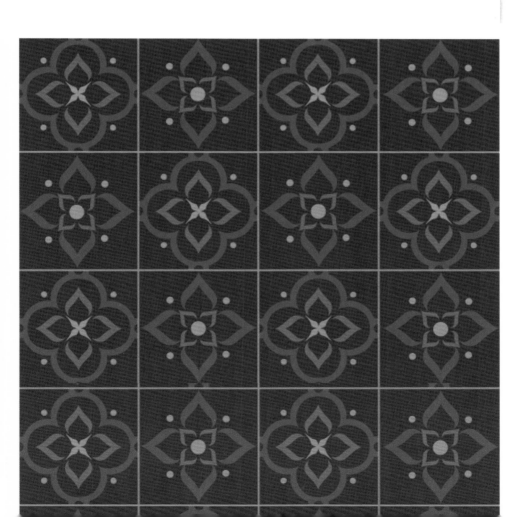

studio chavez

www.studiochavez.com
WEB

ekim@studiochavez.com
E-MAIL

415.577.4070
TEL

121

KARA MANN

KATIE MARCHESI

E: KMARCHESI@KARAMANN.COM
V: 312.893.7592

KARA MANN
119 WEST HUBBARD . FIFTH FLOOR
CHICAGO, ILLINOIS 60610
T: 312.893.7590 . **F:** 312.893.7591
W: WWW.KARAMANN.COM

Info
For this renowned interior-design consultancy, which produces sleek and comfortable environments for residential and commercial settings, Chris May created a custom "wallpaper" pattern. Complete with edgy skulls, the pattern playfully blends contemporary aesthetics with decorative traditions.

For
Kara Mann_
Interior Designers_
Chicago, USA

Design
Chris May_
Telemetre

SARAHSHAOUL

t 503.888.0161
f 503.335.3972
e sarah@sarahshaoul.com
www.sarahshaoul.com

Design
Ian Lynam_
Ian Lynam Design

For
Sarah Shaoul_
Small Business
Consultant_
Portland, USA

Info
Printed litho on recycled white card stock, this business
card combines a pattern inspired by Japanese textiles
from the 1950s with the "colour scheme of summer".

www.thisiscrap.org

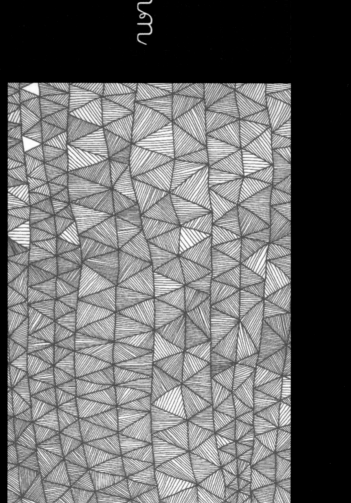

Design
Patrick Carvalho
Dumont_
This Is Crap

For
This Is Crap_
Designer_
Brussels, Belgium

Info
A lifelong doodler, Patrick Carvalho Dumont remembers: "My parents drove us all over Brazil in their car, so, to keep the noise down and stop me from bugging my little sister, they stuck a pad and some colouring pens in my hands, and voilà" Today he's still drawing, and sharing his sketchbook with the world.

Design
Matthew McCarthy_
Edith Prakoso_
Indie Ladan_
Clear Design

For
Twisted Tastes_
Catering and
Hospitality
Training_
Melbourne,
Australia

Info
Turning letterforms into a logo: take all those "t" combinations
and make them into a "marque" reminiscent of helping hands
and teamwork.

twisted.tastes

twisted.tastes

sally ridden (bmhv)
catering events training

sally@twistedtastes.com.au
twistedtastes.com.au
m 0413 061 638

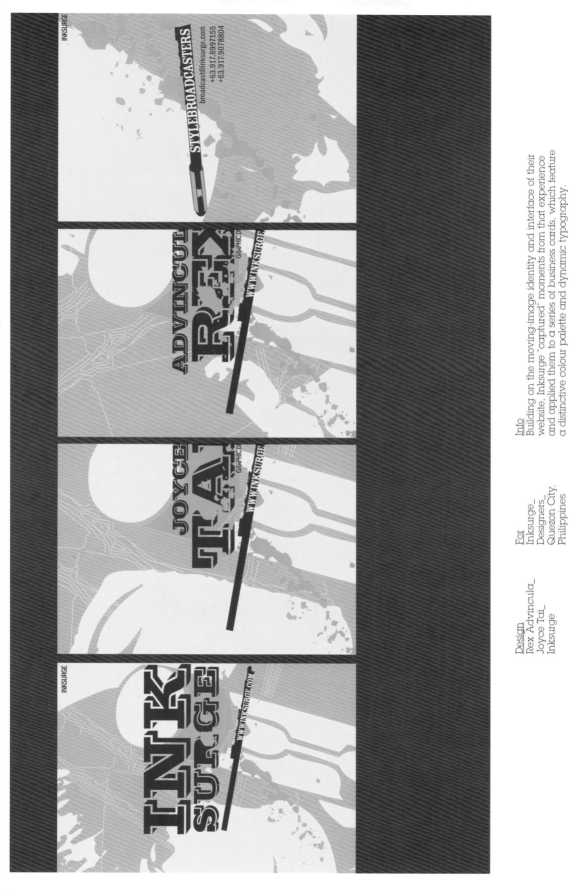

Info
Building on the moving-image identity and interface of their website, Inksurge 'captured' moments from that experience and applied them to a series of business cards, which feature a distinctive colour palette and dynamic typography.

For
Inksurge_
Designers_
Quezon City,
Philippines

Design
Rex Advincula_
Joyce Tai_
Inksurge

127

Design
Keith Stephenson_
Absolute Zero Degrees

For
Absolute Zero
Degrees_
Designers_
London, UK

Info
Using recycled card stock and litho printing. Absolute Zero Degrees showcase a range of patterns developed for both design projects and their own brand of wallpapers and accessories. This set of business cards features eight patter the reverse is personalized by staff members.

absolutezero°

| Address | Telephone |

10 Empress Mews
Kenbury Street
London
SE5 9BT

+44 (0)20 77376767

www.absolutezerodegrees.com

my name is: Keith Stephenson

here's my number: 07989 159969

keith@absolutezerodegrees.com

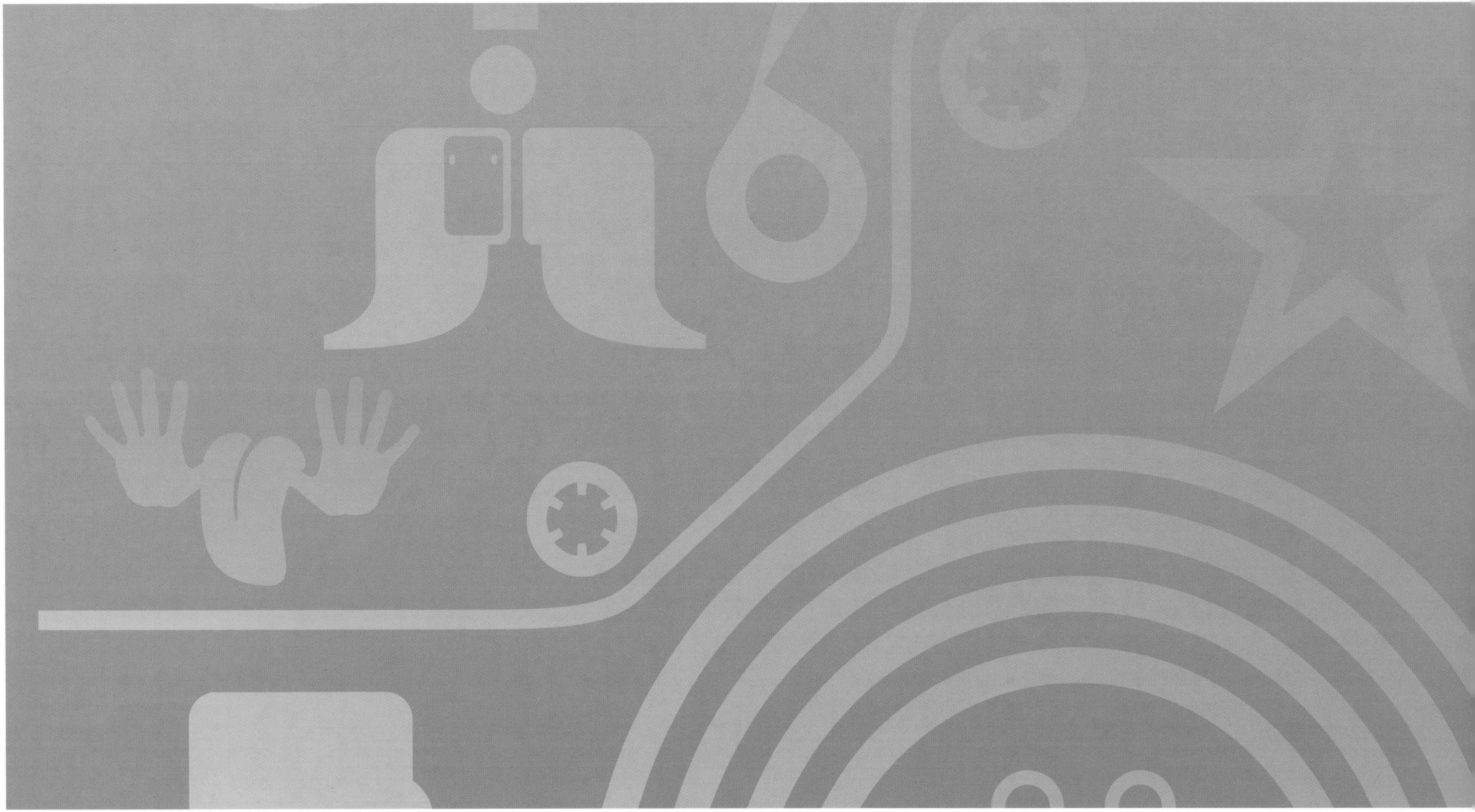

Design
Julien Crouïgneau_
Design June

For
Design June_
Designers_
Montmorency,
France

Info
Arranging an all-over pattern from a profusion of diverse
illustrations, Design June hint at the creative overload they offer.

julien crouïgneau
julien@designjune.com
06 81 43 34 83

designjune
1bis avenue de la folie
95160 montmorency
france

+33 (0)9 53 83 96 01
designjune.com

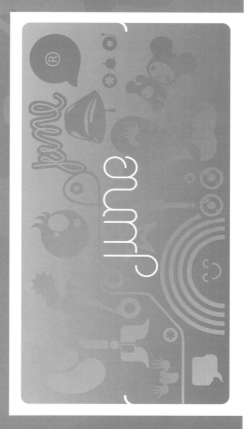

june ®

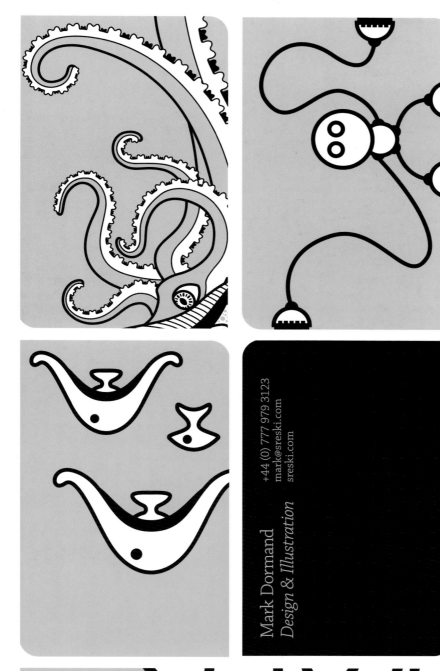

Mark Dormand
Design & Illustration

+44 (0) 777 979 3123
mark@sreski.com
sreski.com

Design
Mark Dormand

For
Mark Dormand_
Designer/
Illustrator_
Manchester, UK

Info
On one side it's a minimalist business card; on the flipside there's an explosion of vibrant colour and a series of quirky characters, creatures and patterns, illustrated in Mark Dormand's signature fluid style. The series is designed to be collected.

Design
Neil McFarland_
Paris Hair

For
Paris Hair_
Illustrator,
London, UK

Info
This illustrator's world is peopled by the most fantastical creatures, all big eyes and wild hair – there's more than a nod here to Japanese manga. McFarland's card features some of his beguiling and mysterious imagery.

Neil McFarland
parishair.com

neil@parishair.com
+44 (0)7811 453 226

Biganimal Studio Truman Brewery 91 Brick Lane London E1 6QL

Richard Hogg
0787 581 0754
richard@h099.com
www.h099.com
(aitch, nought, ninetynine.com)

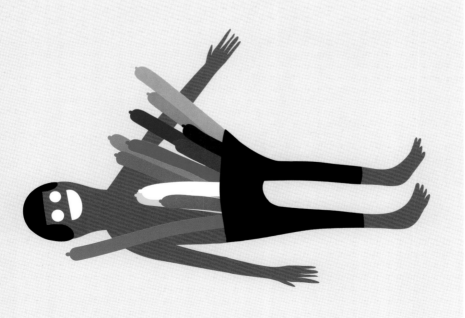

Design
Richard Hogg

For
Richard Hogg_
Designer/Illustrator_
London, UK

Info
This designer/illustrator incorporates colourful, witty image-making into all sorts of design projects, including live-action and animated films. His 'balloons' are funny, irreverent and sexy – an enviable combination – and act as a versatile, ever-changing logo.

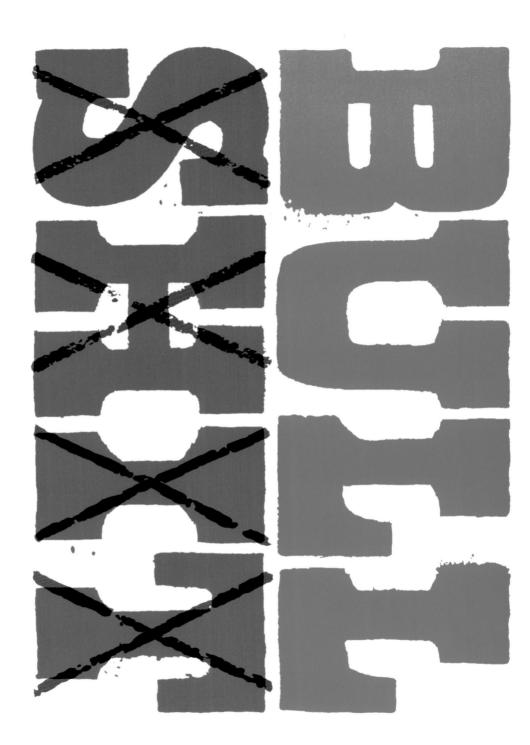

Design
Andy Smith

For
Andy Smith_
Illustrator_
Hastings, UK

Info
These large-format cards (both litho and screenprinted) are intended to show off Smith's speciality: hand-drawn typography in the context of print-friendly illustrations. Smith is an avid screenprinter and produces short-run illustrated books.

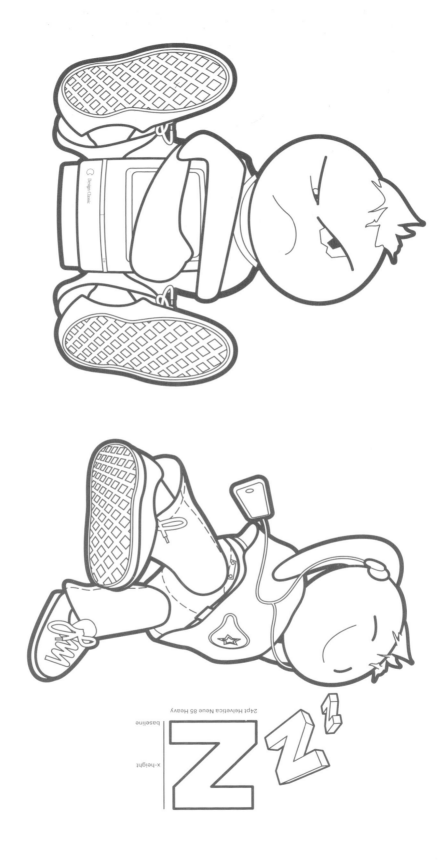

24pt Helvetica Neue 85 Heavy

baseline

x-height

GraphicPull

Info
A series of three drawings of a cute character (is it the designer's alter ego?) who literally dreams design and is very attached to his Apple Mac. The reverse of the card is saturated with vibrant spot fluorescent ink.

For
GraphicPull_
Designer
Woking, UK

Design
Richard Hunt_
GraphicPull

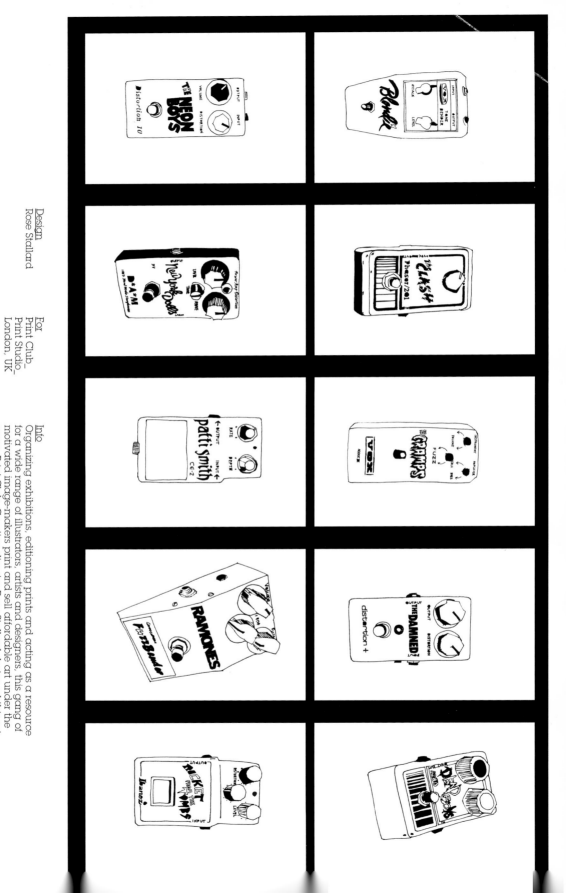

Design
Rose Stallard

For
Print Club_
Print Studio_
London, UK

Info
Organizing exhibitions, editioning prints and acting as a resource for a wide range of illustrators, artists and designers, this gang of motivated image-makers print and sell affordable art under the name Print Club. Creative director Rose Stallard designed this set of business cards featuring customized guitar pedals for rock and roll heroes.

PRINT CLUB

ROSE STALLARD
CREATIVE DIRECTOR.

T 0044 (0)7780 853 757
E rose@printclublondon.com
W www.printclublondon.com

Unit 3
Millers Avenue, Dalston
London E8 2DS

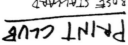

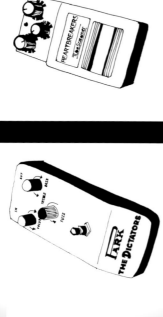

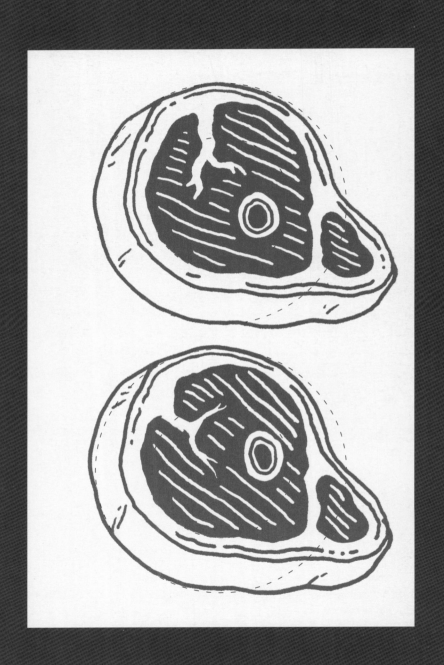

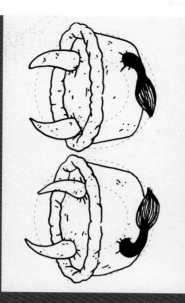

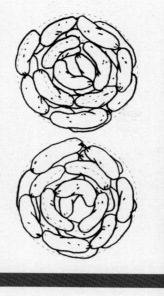

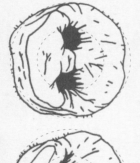

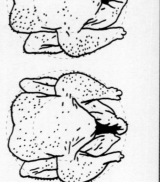

VE **PURE GR**

6-8 Smithfields
London EC3 8GH
www.puregroove.co.uk

Ziad Nashnush
Manager
+44 (0)20 7345 3455
+44 (0)7985 231097
ziad@puregroove.co.uk

Design
Patrick Duffy_
No Days Off
Illustration
Chris Graham

For
Pure Groove_
Record Shop and
Music Publishing
Company_
London, UK

Info
The concentric dotted lines represent the double "o" in "groove"; this element and the contact details are pre-printed two-colour litho. The meaty elements (also circular, and comic-book funny) are rubber-stamped onto each card. The meat theme reminds customers that the shop is located in Smithfields, the home of London's wholesale meat market.

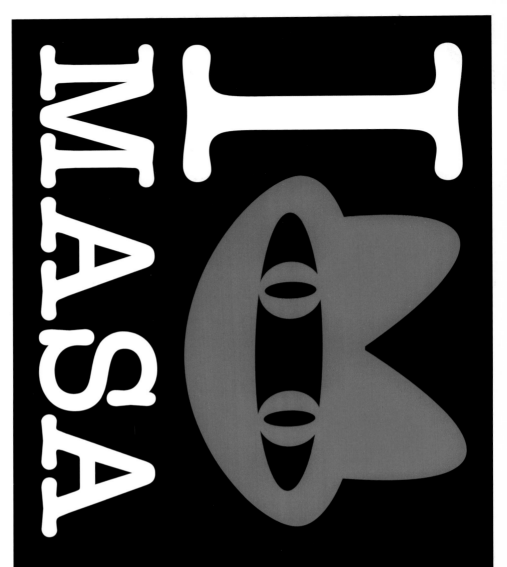

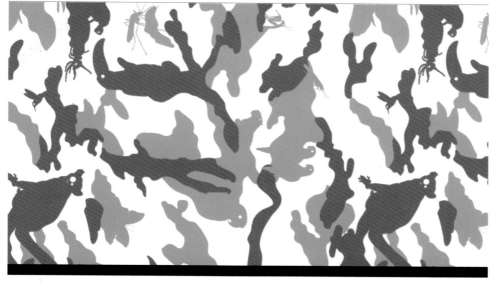

ART DIRECTION
DESIGN & ILLUSTRATION
FOR ENTERTAINMENT, MUSIC,
FASHION AND URBAN / YOUTH
ORIENTED CULTURE CLIENTS.

hello@masa.com.ve
www.masa.com.ve

For
MASA_
Illustrator
Caracas, Venezuela

Design
MASA

Info
A series of large-format business cards (50x90mm/2x3.5in),
printed on glasé paper, showcases the diversity of MASA's
personal and commercial work, and includes his spin on
the "I Heart" logo – MASA substitutes a cute, cat-like critter!
The "instant" aesthetic of the logo also hints at his street-art
influences and experiences.

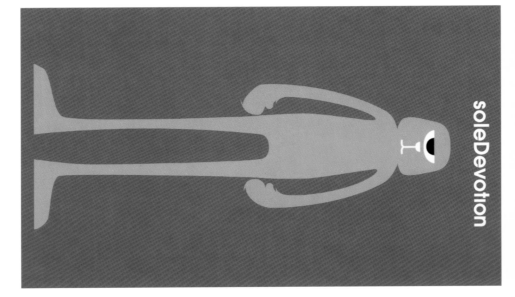

soleDevotion

Design
Matthew McCarthy_
Edith Prakoso_
Clear Design

For
SoleDevotion,
Shoe Importers
and Distributors_
Melbourne,
Australia

Info
With this set of four business cards, the aim was to mix fun and
sophistication, introducing street style to high fashion, since this
shoe import business deals with all styles of "must have" footwear.

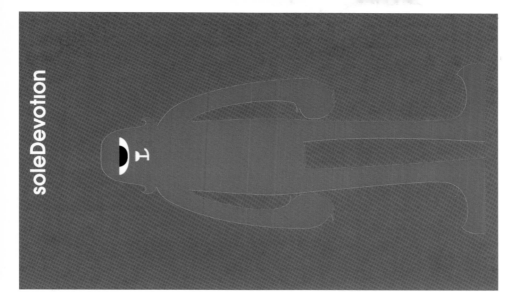

soleDevotion

soleDevotion

124 greville st prahran 3181
store@soleDevotion·com·au
soleDevotion·com·au

T +61 3 9510 6844
F +61 3 9510 6268

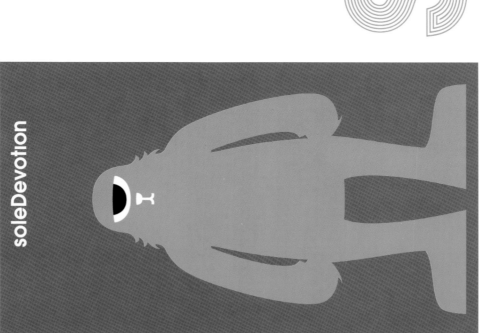

soleDevotion

148

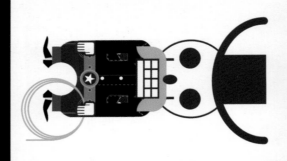

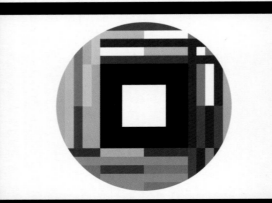

CHRISTIAN@CHRISTIANMONTENEGRO.COM.AR

Design
Laura Varsky

Illustration
Christian Montenegro

For
Christian Montenegro_
Illustrator_
Buenos Aires,
Argentina

Info
This series of business cards for the renowned illustrator, Christian Montenegro, features a selection of his whimsical, elegant, fanciful and fun drawings, reproduced using just two colours.

WWW.**CHRISTIANMONTENEGRO**.COM.AR

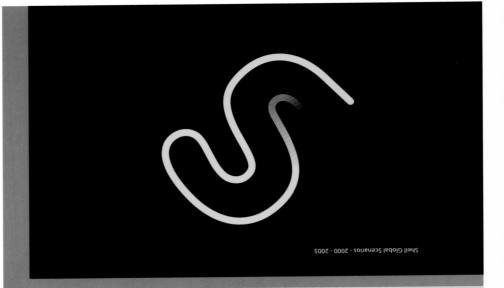

Shell Global Scenarios - 2000 - 2005

Design
Peter Grundy_
Grundini

For
Grundini_
Designer_
London, UK

Architects language poster - 1989

Info
Famed as an information designer with a witty sense of style,
Peter Grundy uses this set of cards to announce the renaming
of his studio and the launch of a major publication.

YTD
3 YR
5 YR

Total
return

30
25
20
15
10
5

Bloomberg magazine infographics - 1994

151

Peter Grundy
Art&design

Studio 69
1 Town Meadow
Brentford
Middlesex TW8 0BQ
UK

peter@grundini.com
+44 (0)20 8384 1076
www.grundini.com

Associate:
Tilly Northedge

Opening hours:
8am to 4pm
Monday to Friday

Alien language poster - 1990

VW Save Fuel advertisement for BMP - 2005

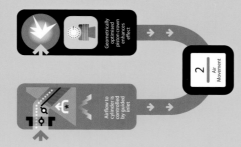

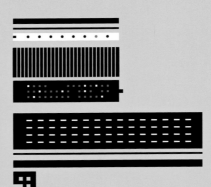

City won poster - 1998

Book dividers for Communications Development - 1998

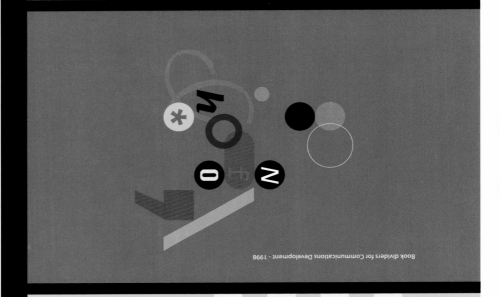

Enigma identity - 2000

BT Internet characters for AMV BBDO - 2000

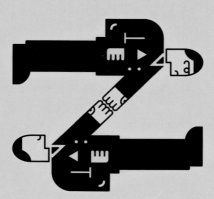

Simpson Molloy identity - 1984

Ophthalmology Institute - 1995

Design
Craig Holden
Feinberg

Photography
Gabriele Schiavon_
Christina Fölmer

Illustration
Nico Vascellari

Creative Direction
Omar Vulpinari_
Fabrica

For
Fabrica,
Benetton's Research
Communication
Centre_
Treviso, Italy

Info
Taken from a set of six business cards, these examples show the use of both photography and illustration by members of the creative team at Fabrica. The entire stationery system comprises multiple images, reflecting the multidisciplinary approach of this research institution.

F A B R I C A

Fabrica Spa
Via Ferrarezza
Catena di Villorba Tv
31020 Italy

T. +39 0422 516111
F. +39 0422 609088

Omar Vulpinari
Visual Communication
Consultant

Direct line +39 0422 516235
omar.vulpinari@fabrica.it

start.

Michael Dorrian
Art Director

Start Creative Limited
2 Sheraton Street
Soho
London
W1F 8BH

T : +44 (0)20 7269 0101
D : +44 (0)20 7269 0148
M : +44 (0)7802 610 054
E : michael@startcreative.co.uk
W : www.startcreative.co.uk

Design
Start Creative

For
Start Creative_
Designers,
London, UK

Info
Each staff member at this large creative consultancy was asked to choose an image – either of a person, place, object or quirky gadget – to illustrate their personalized business card. The black-and-white "street style" treatment and the hilarious quotes create an aesthetic that is edgy, fun and in-your-face.

Design
Damien Weighill

For
Damien Weighill_
Illustrator,
London, UK

Info
Irreverent and precocious, Weighill describes this as
"Her Majesty the Queen and her luxurious moustache
on a business card". It always gets a reaction.

Damien Weighill

illustration
(+44) 07920 844 545
DAMIEN@DAMIENWEIGHILL.COM

doodleroom

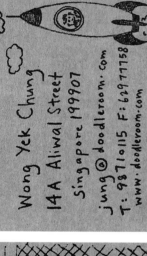

Wong Yek Chung
14A Aliwal Street
Singapore 199907
jung@doodleroom.com
T: 9871 0115 F: 6291711158
www.doodleroom.com

9875 2555

Fire wee

SKIp work for a whine about life at 14A Aliwal St, Singapore 199907. Cup a bored black and eyeball the job sheets peeling off our hot fax 62977758. Notice all the triplenumbers on this card ey? Go on a hunch. Take a chance on us. Quick! Bet on a bet-ter life. No? next time then. Yes! Remember me-mail your best pal val@doodleroom.com & oodles of good gravy Karma will flow forth. And if you send us struggling creatives here a fat cheque, we will gladly immortalise you in our sticky web of fame at www.doodleroom.com

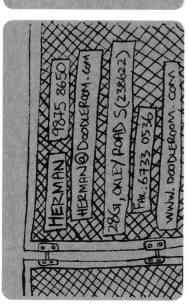

HERMAN 9845 8650
HERMAN@DOODLEROOM.COM
286, OXLEY ROAD S(238622)
FAX: 6733 0536
WWW.DOODLEROOM.COM

HERMAN 98758650
14A Aliwal Street Singapore 199907
Fax: 62977758
herman@doodleroom.com
www.doodleroom.com

Info
Each member of staff at this agency was invited to "doodle" their own business card design so as to represent their personality, their aesthetic preferences or simply their thoughts at that particular moment.

For
Doodleroom_
Advertising/Design
Agency_
Singapore

Design
Herman Ho_
Valerie Wee_
Chung Wong_
Doodleroom

POSITION 09

POSITION 06

POSITION 04

POSITION 07

Design
Agathe Jacquillat_
Tomi Vollauschek_
FL@33

For
Matelsom_
Online Bed
Supplier,
Nanterre, France

Info
A custom-designed font and informational line drawings of sleep poses provide an aesthetically refined graphic with scientific overtones for this online supplier of beds and mattresses. Each employee chooses their own favourite sleep position for their business card.

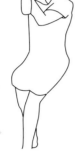

POSITION 05

POSITION 11

POSITION 09

malik boudagga   responsable grands comptes

P +33 (0)6 20 06 54 26
T +33 (0)1 55 66 06 48
F +33 (0)1 55 66 06 68
E malik.sc@matelsom.com

18-22 rue d'arras
92000 nanterre
www.matelsom.com

matelsom
N1 DE LA LITERIE EN LIGNE

POSITION 08

Info
Showcasing his flawless draughtsmanship, Sam Green's visually arresting business card features a drawing investigating the "astral plane".

For
Sam Green_
Illustrator_
London, UK

Design
Sam Green

Design
Götz Gramlich_
GGGrafik

For
Claus Geiss_
Photographer_
Germany

Info
Combining numerous illustrative elements into fantastical compositions, this set of eight business cards features animals, plants, letters, inkblots and abstract calligraphy, which also appear on the reverse of this photographer's stationery.

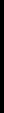

Fotografie Claus Geiss
+49 [0]176.22844924
clausgeiss.com
ben@clausgeiss.com

164

Design
Therese Vandling

For
Therese Vandling_
Designer/Illustrator_
London, UK

Info
Comprising slightly smaller than average business cards – four are cut from a standard postcard – this series is entitled "The Unfinished Body", based on a quote by Mikhail Bakhtin. Investigating his definition of the "grotesque ornament", where life and death, in their animal, plant and human forms, are all intertwined. Therese Vandling created a "grotesque" typeface from obscure cut-ups and abstract patterns.

Therese Vandling MA RCA
therese@vandling.co.uk
therese.vandling@alumni.rca.ac.uk
+ 44 (0) 795 060 1004
www.vandling.co.uk

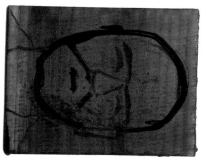

Alfonso X el Sabio, 27 6H
03001   Alicante
pepetalavera@hotmail.com
+ 3 4 6 9 9 2 2 0 0 2 5

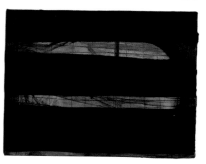

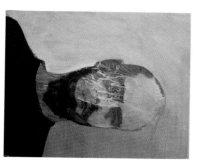

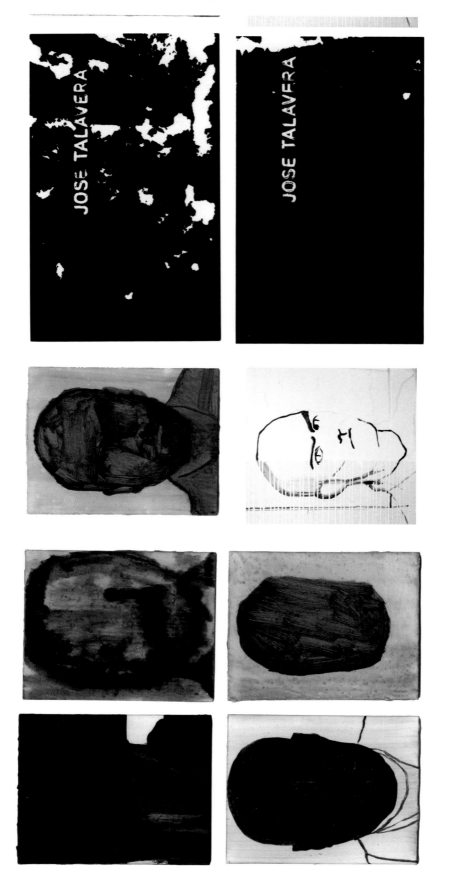

Design
Diego Hurtado
de Mendoza

For
José Talavera_
Painter_
Alicante, Spain

Info
Starting with a group of José Talavera's self-portraits, Diego Hurtado
de Mendoza added an accidental element, a technical glitch, to the
reproduction process. Produced using a plasticized paper with a thermo-
stamping printer, each copy is slightly different. "I achieved this effect by
studying the printer's technical manual," explains the designer, "to find out
what shouldn't be done with certain inks and methods."

Design/Photography
Agathe Jacquillat_
Toni Vollauschek_
FL@33

For
FL@33_
Designers,
London, UK

Info
The fifth in a series of promotional postcard-size business cards from
FL@33. "Shadows" presents a montage of passers-by photographed from
the Eiffel Tower. Playing with scale, foreshortening and viewpoint, the
result is an intriguing composition that leaves you wanting to know
more about these individuals and groups, and their relationships.

Shadows, Passers by seen from Eiffel Tower, 2003

flat33

flat33
multi-disciplinary design studio
for visual communication

Founding Directors:
Agathe Jacquillat MA (RCA)
Tomi Vollauschek MA (RCA)

Email:
contact@flat33.com

http://www.
flat33.com
stereohype.com
bzzzpeek.com

Studio:
+44 (0)20 7168 7090
59 Britton Street
London
EC1M 5UU
United Kingdom

Design
Sabine Kobel

Photography
HB Lankowitz

For
HB Lankowitz,
Photographers_
Traufkirchen,
Germany

Info
Graphic designer Sabine Kobel works closely with the photography duo known as HB Lankowitz; they are in fact two people disguised as one and using a bogus name. For this card Kobel cut-up discarded prints to create a composite portrait of the duo, while playing with the media convention for masking identity.

hb lankowitz

Brigitta Reuter + Hubert Hasler
Fotografie

Ritter-Hilprant-Str. 8
82024 Taufkirchen
Tel.: 089 - 21 75 53 38
Mobil: + 49 (0) 152 - 03 61 76 14

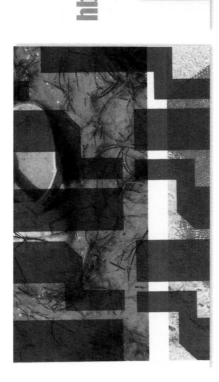

'i-am' associates

identity
environments
culture

the old school house
66 leonard street
london ec2a 4lw

tel +44 (0) 20 7613 4114
fax +44 (0) 20 7613 4224
mobile 07976 573 235
email pete@i-amonline.com
web www.i-amonline.com

'i-am'

Pete Champion
pioneer

am i in tune?
am i plugged in?
am i having fun?

'i-am' associates

innovation identity experiences

'i-am'

Tim Jeffrey
professional shopper

As a young boy rope knit jumpers became a big part of my life until I managed to confiscate my mothers knitting needles. From then on choice became an option and shops became an attraction. With shopping came mobility and with mobility came my love of cars. Shops and cars, shops and cars......

'i-am' associates

innovation identity experiences

the old school house
66 leonard street
london ec2a 4lw

tel +44 (0) 20 7613 4114
fax +44 (0) 20 7613 4224
mobile 07768 602 844
email tim@i-amonline.com
web www.i-amonline.com

'i-am'

'i-am' associates

innovation identity experiences

the old school house
66 leonard street
london ec2a 4lw

tel +44 (0) 20 7613 4114
fax +44 (0) 20 7613 4224
email claire@i-amonline.com
web www.i-amonline.com

'i-am'

Claire Parkinson
miss motivator

little women meets
moulin rouge
loves dressing up
likes partying down
synchronized swimmer
shoes shoes shoes
'sparky parky'
mary poppins on crack

'i-am' associates

innovation identity experiences

the old school house
66 leonard street
london ec2a 4lw

tel +44 (0) 20 7613 4114
fax +44 (0) 20 7613 4224
mobile 07887 702 089

email george@i-amonline.com
web www.i-amonline.com

George Simkin
potato man

from the peoples
republic of Cork
banjo perfectionist
fake jaw line
sketchbook lover
happiest when fed
bottle of wine...
doin fine

'i-am'

'i-am' associates

**identity
environments
culture**

the old school house
66 leonard street
london ec2a 4lw

tel +44 (0) 20 7613 4114
fax +44 (0) 20 7613 4224
mobile 07951 866 145

email simon@i-amonline.com
web www.i-amonline.com

'i-am'

is: compassionate,
cheery, bald
does: listen well,
think hard
create beautifully
done: amazon trekking,
thailand diving,
new zealand free fall
hates: rules, marzipan, lies
loves: the ocean, new shoes,
wheelies

Simon May
sparkler

'i-am'

'i-am' associates

**identity
environments
culture**

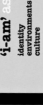

the old school house
66 leonard street
london ec2a 4lw

tel +44 (0) 20 7613 4114
fax +44 (0) 20 7613 4224
mobile 07976 744 862

email jon@i-amonline.com
web www.i-amonline.com

1965, left hander
dad, metrosexual
addicted to shopping
showjump champion
wild gastronome
callipygian forms
high boiling point
big plans

Jonathan Blakeney
experientor

'i-am'

Info
This dynamic design consultancy treats its staff members to personalized business cards featuring witty copy, an archive photo and a cute illustration; they break the ice and introduce the talent.

For
I-Am Associates_
Designers_
London, UK

Design
Pero Trivunovic_
I-Am Associates

'i-am' associates
identity
environments
culture

the old school house
66 leonard street
london ec2a 4lw

tel +44 (0) 20 7613 4114
fax +44 (0) 20 7613 4224
mobile 07989 583 012
email james@i-amonline.com
web www.i-amonline.com

'i-am'
James Coates
innovator

no north/south divide
a true midlander;
right side thinker!
love jazzy, funky,
techi, disco beats.
pub snug &
cheesy moments.
if you're gonna be
a bear be a grizzly!
man bag enthusiast

'i-am' associates
innovation identity experiences

'i-am'
Jolyon Nott
transformer

100g/4oz original thinking,
100g/4oz innovation,
50g/2oz inspiration,
175g/6oz technical ability,
the zest of some true
bloody mindedness,
2.5 pints London Pride,
200g/8oz accumulated
knowledge,
300C/400F/gas mark 4
until nicely golden.

'i-am' associates
innovation identity experiences

the old school house
66 leonard street
london ec2a 4lw.

tel +44 (0) 20 7613 4114
fax +44 (0) 20 7613 4224
email jolyon@i-amonline.com
web www.i-amonline.com

'i-am' associates
innovation identity experiences

the old school house
66 leonard street
london ec2a 4lw

tel +44 (0) 20 7613 4114
fax +44 (0) 20 7613 4224
mobile 07719 596 863
email ben@i-amonline.com
web www.i-amonline.com

born in 1973
love 007 and biscuits
strictly jeans & trainers
cheeky when provoked
strong hairline
always aim to please
jack of all trades
master of some

'i-am'
Ben Russell
graphics & stuff

limROCK to londON
chicken katsu curry
can't use chopsticks
japanese films
can't speak japanese
lover of music
can't sing a note

Patrick Cusack
ché pablo

'i-am'

'i-am' associates
innovation identity experiences

the old school house
66 leonard street
london ec2a 4lw

tel +44 (0) 20 7613 4114
fax +44 (0) 20 7613 4224
mobile 07783 805 430

email patrick@i-amonline.com
web www.i-amonline.com

'i-am' associates

identity
environments
culture

the old school house
66 leonard street
london ec2a 4lw

tel +44 (0) 20 7613 4114
fax +44 (0) 20 7613 4224
mobile 07835 617 456

email leyla@i-amonline.com
web www.i-amonline.com

seriously unfunny
seaside compatriot
penny-farthing worshipper
sketchy sketcher
100% a twin
instrument playing goddess,
in my dreams.
not a fan of ovens
a tourist

Leyla Weller
thought-collector

'i-am'

200 mile-a-day commuter,
vegetarian fire-eater,
duck keeper, poppy grower,
mean with a ping pong bat,
awful on the trumpet,
interested in sectors
beginning with "F"-
food, farmshops, fashion,
fmcg, funerals, flowers,
fell running & fotography

Bob Bayman
explorer & pathfinder

'i-am'

'i-am' associates

identity
environments
culture

the old school house
66 leonard street
london ec2a 4lw

tel +44 (0) 20 7613 4114
fax +44 (0) 20 7613 4224
mobile 07884 437 571

email bob@i-amonline.com
web www.i-amonline.com

OFFICE OF SIMONE WAGENER
Design & Art Direction

+44 (0) 778 0601 472
office@simonewagener.com
Unit 4, Ridley Road Studios
51-63 Ridley Road Market, London
E8 2NP, UK
www.simonewagener.com

Design/Photography
Simone Wagener

For
Simone Wagener_
Designer_
London, UK

Info
This series of business cards features portraits taken by Simone Wagener, and showcases her multi-tasking approach to design and image-making. Wagener is as much at home behind the camera as she is art-directing, designing and illustrating.

Design
Alter

For
Alter_
Designers_
Melbourne,
Australia

Info
Alter had grown from two to four designers; on their business cards they demonstrate this increase and their connection with music, which includes designing for bands, record labels and venues, and actually playing too. This eye-catching card utilizes two colours, plus a foil and a UV varnish.

Jonathan Wallace

Alter...
151 Union Street
Windsor 3181
Victoria Australia
Phone +61 3 9533 2200
Facsimile +61 3 9533 2299
Mobile +61(0)411 399 910
Email jonathan@alter.com.au
www.alter.com.au

Design/Photography
Martijn Oostra

For
Martijn Oostra_
Designer,
Amsterdam,
the Netherlands

Info
Martijn Oostra incorporates photography, writing and image-making into his art practice and commercial design. By mining the media and looking for beauty in the most banal everyday situations and environments, Oostra creates a dynamic series of photographic business cards.

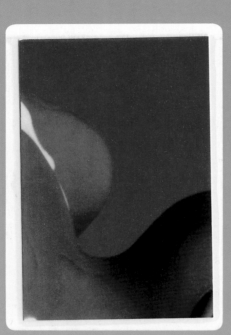

Design
Sabine Kobel

Photography
HB Lankowitz

For
HB Lankowitz_
Photographers_
Taufkirchen,
Germany

Info
In partnership with HB Lankowitz, Sabine Kobel has some
fun creating new series of cards for the photography duo for
successive exhibitions, so as to reflect the content and mood
of each show.

hb lankowitz
Brigitta Reuter + Hubert Hasler
Fotografie

Ritter-Hilprant-Str.8
82024 Taufkirchen
Tel.: 089 - 21 75 53 38
Mobil: + 49 (0) 152 - 03 61 76 14
Email: photo-flores@gmx.net

Info

While art-directing a fashion shoot in Hong Kong, Frank Schouwaerts and team were taken to a local restaurant in the world-famous Wet Market. "There was lots of strange-looking food," he recalls. "When I needed a new business card, I thought: This is a creative picture.' Around the table was a photographer, a model, a make-up artist, the production people... it was one creative table. So the card represents two of my favourite activities, dining and designing."

For
Sterk Water_
Designer_
Antwerp,
Belgium

Design/Photography
Frank Schouwaerts_
Sterk Water

sterk WATER.

GRAPHIC DESIGN
ART DIRECTION
INTERACTIVE

FRANK SCHOUWAERTS
0486/25 74 37

INFO@STERKWATER.BE
WWW.STERKWATER.BE

N	Kelly Hartman	Giles Woodward
E	Fishes@Fishten.Net
T	1.403.228.7959

Design/Photography
Giles Woodward_
Kelly Hartman_
Fishten

For
Fishten_
Designers_
Calgary, Canada

Info
The words "Fish" and "Ten" are photographed in various environments and combined into a flexible, playful identity that uses both sides of the card.

N	Kelly Hartman	Giles Woodward
E	Fishes@Fishten.Net
T	1.403.228.7959

N	Kelly Hartman	Giles Woodward
E	Fishes@Fishten.Net
T	1.403.228.7959

N	Kelly Hartman	Giles Woodward
E	Fishes@Fishten.Net
T	1.403.228.7959

Cybu Richli – Fabienne Burri
Graphic Design

Cybu Richli

Kasimir-Pfyffer-Str. 18a
6003 Luzern — Switzerland

e: c@cybu.ch
t: +41 (0)41 240 44 24
www.c2f.to

2007 — Studio, Kasimir-Pfyffer-Str. 18a, Luzern

2008 — Identity Project, Master of Arts in Interaction Design

2005 — Projects in Chicago and New York

2007 — Project on Wheels, France

2007 — Project on Wheels, France

2007 — Project on Wheels, France

2007 — Project on Wheels, France

Design/Photography_
Cybu Richli
Fabienne Burri

For
Cybu Richli —
Fabienne Burri,
Graphic Design_
Designers_
Luzern, Switzerland

Info
A series of arresting images, featuring completed projects and current briefs, graces this series of business cards, offering an immediate route into discussing this adventurous team's work.

Design
Graphic Thought
Facility

Photography
Angela Moore

Stylist
Sarah May

Origami
Mark Bolitho

For
Oki-Nami_
Japanese
Restaurant,
Brighton, UK

Info
A series of origami creatures are featured in stylized using flowers, foliage and atmospheric lighting to ap various seasons and times of day. The soft colour pa and romantic tableaux echo the relaxed atmospher destination restaurant.

Oki–Nami

ジャパニーズ・ダイニング

Mike Dodd
Director
Mobile 07875 756120
mike@okinami.com

Oki–Nami Restaurant
6 New Road, Brighton BN1 1UF
Telephone bookings 01273 773 777

Oki–Nami Shop
12 York Place, Brighton BN1 4GU
www.okinami.com

JENS KOMOSSA BERLIN

ORANIENBURGER STR. 27 · 10117 BERLIN

WWW.KOMOSSA.NET

FOTO@KOMOSSA.NET

T. (+49) 030.308 72 72 1
F. (+49) 030.308 72 72 2
M. (+49) 0172.307 5 307

JENS KOMOSSA BERLIN

ORANIENBURGER STR. 27 · 10117 BERLIN

WWW.KOMOSSA.NET

FOTO@KOMOSSA.NET

T. (+49) 030.308 72 72 1
F. (+49) 030.308 72 72 2
M. (+49) 0172.307 5 307

JENS KOMOSSA BERLIN

ORANIENBURGER STR. 27 · 10117 BERLIN

WWW.KOMOSSA.NET

FOTO@KOMOSSA.NET

T. (+49) 030.308 72 72 1
F. (+49) 030.308 72 72 2
M. (+49) 0172.307 5 307

<u>Design</u>
Peter Bünnagel_
Barbara Kotte_
Anne-Lene Proff_
Scrollan

<u>For</u>
Jens Komossa_
Photographer_
Berlin, Germany

<u>Info</u>
An evolving series of photo-led business cards showcases Jens Komossa's images and builds into a "deck of cards". Note the rounded corners and patterned reverse inspired by playing-card designs.

JENS KOMOSSA BERLIN

ORANIENBURGER STR. 27 · 10117 BERLIN

WWW.KOMOSSA.NET

FOTO@KOMOSSA.NET

T. (+49) 030.308 72 72 1
F. (+49) 030.308 72 72 2
M.(+49) 0172.307 5 307

Design
Matt Kelley—
One Lucky Guitar

For
Vorderman
Photography—
Photography
Studio,
Roanoke, USA

Info
A simple white-out-of-black business card is made memorable by the addition of perforations to produce a "portable cropping tool".

Design
Karen Knecht_
KonnectDesign

For
Ron Berg
Photography_
Photographer_
Kansas City, USA

Info
A folded and die-cut card gives this versatile photographer a double image: cool and restrained on one side, while the reverse is fun and intriguing, featuring cropped images framed by a speech bubble.

Design
Danny Jenkins_
Andy Hussey_
Thirteen

For
Plymouth Arts
Centre_
Cultural Venue_
Plymouth, UK

Info
This set of business cards features a pair of graphic elements:
die-cut geometric patterns teamed with a palette of rich colours
that are hidden and revealed via the folded format. The
end result is a sophisticated yet edgy identity for this busy
cultural venue.

Design
Dan Moore_
Studio Output

For
Shine
Communications_
Public Relations
Agency_
London, UK

Info
The fold-over format allows for these personalized cards
to be used as place-setting markers during meetings, while
the contrasting matt ground and spot varnish text creates
a distinct "shine".

Melissa Morton Hicks

387'b King Street London W6 9NJ
Mobile: +44 (0)7973 259 688
Telephone: +44 (0)20 8748 3042
Fax: +44 (0)20 8748 7634
Email: melissa@isis-productions.com
www.isis-productions.com

Design
Natasha Shah_
Chris Hilton_
Design Friendship

For
ISIS Productions_
Film Production_
Company_
London, UK

Info
Design Friendship designed an iconic logo and used it here
to great effect. Combining two spot colours and a die-cut on
brilliant white uncoated card stock, it functions as a word, a
symbol and an abstract pattern, and intriguingly can be read
even in negative.

Info
Offset-printed onto perforated card stock, this "concertina" business card folds into a stack of six. "I wanted to make a statement," explains the designer, "about the ongoing debate on specialization by saying, yes, I'm a graphic designer, I communicate through many media, and don't restrict me to just one thing. Everyone always smiles and thanks me for six cards, especially when they read them and reach the last one!"

For
Diego Hurtado
de Mendoza_
Designer_
Madrid, Spain

Design
Diego Hurtado
de Mendoza

Design
Bunch

For
Kapulica Studio_
Event Production_
Zagreb, Croatia

Info
The 'K' (taken from the client's name) starts out as a simple black-
and-white logo. For these business cards, the letter is die-cut and
pops up to reveal a series of different mood-setting images.

Design
Jakob Straub_
Winnie Becker_
Grafisches Gestalten
Berlin, Germany

For
Aurel Scheibler_
Art Gallery_

Info
This eye-catching but enigmatic business card is based on the floorplan of a new gallery. Through folding, the shape becomes further abstracted.

PETER AND PAUL

Unit R9a, Riverside Block
Sheaf Bank Business Park
Prospect Road, Sheffield
S2 3EN, England
Phone: 0114 255 6119
Mobile: 07931 556 125
www.peterandpaul.co.uk
peter@peterandpaul.co.uk

Design
Peter and Paul

For
Peter and Paul_
Designers_
Sheffield, UK

Info
Using a textured stock reminiscent of stencil matboard, this die-cut card works in two ways, depending on whether Peter or Paul is presenting it.

allies

CREATIVE DIRECTOR

Susanna Cook

Susanna Cook
108 Great Portland Street
Fitzrovia
London W1W 6PG

T. +44 (0)20 7636 3377
F. +44 (0)20 7299 7930

www.**allies**design.com

susanna@alliesdesign.com

Design
Susanna Cook_
Allies

For
Allies_
Designers,
London, UK

Info
Depicting a selection of invitations, flyers and cards lined up on a mantelpiece, this business card displays the eclectic sources of inspiration that Allies enjoy, and offers a window into the designers' world. The folded format and the staff members' signatures echo the display by approximating the intimacy of a greetings card.

the
apartment.
& BERLIN &
TALENT &
FASHION &
STOCKHOLM
& NSFW &
FOOD & ARC-
HITECTURE

the
apartment.
& HONGKO...
& MOVIES &
MARKETING &
SHANGHAI &
SUCKS &
ARCHITEC-
TURE & ART

...@
theapt.com
P.212.219.3661
ext.__-

Info
A bound tablet of 96 leaves, each booklet contains eight sets of 12 different cards featuring contact details and keywords, all enlivened with a dynamic mix of florid ampersands and bold type.

For
The Apartment_
Designers_
New York, USA

Design
Peter Crnokrak_
±

Creative Direction
Stefan Boublil

Design
Ben Levitz_
Ned Wright_
Steve Jockisch_
Jason Strong_
Joel Stacy_
Riley Kane_
Dane Roberts

Creative Direction
William Jurewicz_
Space150

For
Space150_
Designers/
Los Angeles/
Minneapolis/
New York, USA

Info
Space150 change their visual identity – from business cards to name plate – every 150 days. Teams of designers work with printers and suppliers to investigate new methods and materials and create an ever-evolving identity. Copywriting is also an important element, with one card summing up this ambitious endeavour: "The Future Feels Good". These virtuoso cards are embossed, die-cut or even stamped from metal.

Info
As everyone in the film and advertising business knows, a
necessary evil of post-production work is sitting around in small,
dark rooms until the early hours. As a result you need the best
biscuits to accompany all that tea-drinking. This plateful of
digitally enhanced business cards wittily reflects that offering!

Design
Mark Denton_
Mark Denton
Design
Typography_
Andy Dymock

For
Nice Biscuits_
Digital Post-
Production
Company_
London, UK

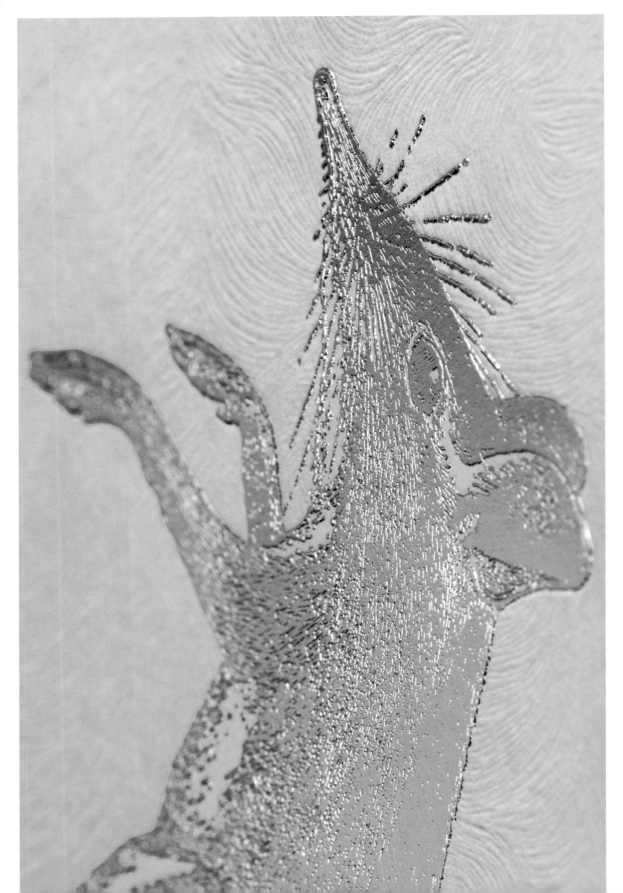

ASD LIONHEART

Nick Sutherland-Dodd

6 D'Arblay Street, London,
W1F 8DN
www.asdlionheart.com
T: +44 (0) 20 7437 3898
M: +44 (0) 7785 255 885
E: nick@asdlionheart.com

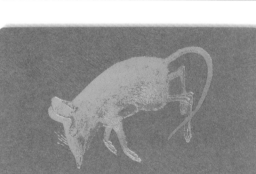

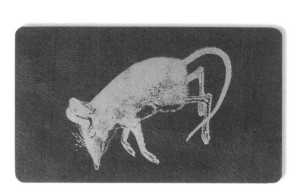

Design
Matt Blease
Creative Direction
Julian Dickinson_
Nick Steel
HarrimanSteel

For
ASD Lionheart_
Post-Production
Company_
London, UK

Info
Using embossed card stock, muted colours and gold foil, this set of business cards was designed to evoke a sense of tradition and value, teamed with strong, contemporary typography. The cute rodent adds a hint of humour.

Design
Despina Bournele_
Di Depux

Typography/Printing
Panos Davias

For
Di Depux_
Designer
Athens, Greece

Info
Having an autobiographical set of die-cut cards, in various materials and metallic inks hung on a key-chain with a Perspex heart, allows Despina Bournele to select just the right one for each recipient. "I love my job so I called this project 'Design With All My Love'," she explains. "As for the colours – pink because I'm girly, gold for glamour and the precious heart."

214

Design
Stiletto NYC

For
Cenerino,
Children's Fashion
Boutique,
Bassano del Grappa,
Italy

Info
Asked to design an identity, including business cards that doubled as swing tags and bag closures, Stiletto NYC differentiated this children's clothes shop by focusing on magical, super-sweet imagery and creative applications. They used die-cuts, a subtle palette of pinks and browns, different stocks (from board to tissues) and a collection of butterfly motifs.

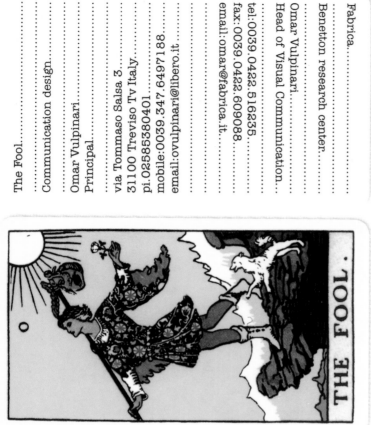

The Fool...............................

Communication design....................

Omar Vulpinari..........................
Principal...............................

via Tommaso Salsa 3.....................
31100 Treviso Tv Italy..................
pi.02585380401..........................
mobile:0039.347.6497188.................
email:ovulpinari@libero.it..............

Fabrica.................................
Benetton research center................

Omar Vulpinari..........................
Head of Visual Communication............

tel:0039.0422.516235....................
fax:0039.0422.609088....................
email:omar@fabrica.it...................

THE FOOL.

Info
Using the format of an illustrated tarot card, this double-headed
business card demonstrates Omar Vulpinari's two roles as a
communication designer and a member of the team at Fabrica.
The illustration is sourced from a set of Art Nouveau illustrations.

For
The Fool_
Designer_
Treviso, Italy

Design
Omar Vulpinari_
The Fool

COLIN GREGG

020 7436 5191

SIMON LEVENE

020 7436 5191

GUY MANWARING

020 7436 5191

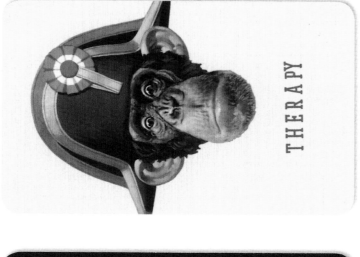

THERAPY

MALCOLM VENVILLE

020 7436 5191

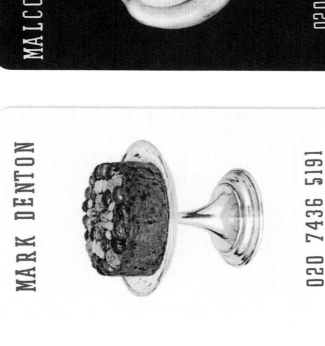

MARK DENTON

020 7436 5191

Design
Mark Denton
Design

Typography
Andy Dymock

Photography
Charlie Crane

For
Therapy Films_
Film Production
Company_
London, UK

Info
The mad monkey is the mascot of Therapy Films, the sister company of Mark Denton Design, and appears on all stationery. The other symbols in this series of business cards (printed four-colour on textured card stock) offer a range of slang terms for insanity to say: "Get some Therapy!" Mark Denton calls it "a twisted identity"!

Design/Illustration
Adam Larson_
Adam&Co.

For
Laura Albert_
Writer_
New York, USA

Info
The elaborate hoax of J.T. LeRoy rocked the literary world. The writer behind the pseudonym, Laura Albert, has since been fighting to demonstrate that her actions were motivated by art and not fraud. Adam Larson's elaborately decorative card (printed with two colours and gold foil) presents Albert as a "Literary Terrorist", albeit gagged.

Design
Steve Payne_
Studio Output

For
Bluu_
Nottingham, UK

Info
This series of business cards, which double as membership cards, is based on a deck of playing cards, with rounded edges and imagery that reference vintage nudie playing cards, ideal for Strip Poker, overlaid with night-time neon and bar icons.

Info
This design partnership specializes in producing limited-edition silk-screen prints. By utilizing cut-down, rejected prints as business cards (adding contact information to the reverse), they're guaranteed an ever-changing visual identity – and a large series of super-tactile, collectable cards.

For
Revenge Is Sweet_
Designers_
Melbourne,
Australia

Design
Lee Owens_
Angelique Piliere_
Revenge Is Sweet

222

REVENGE IS SWEET

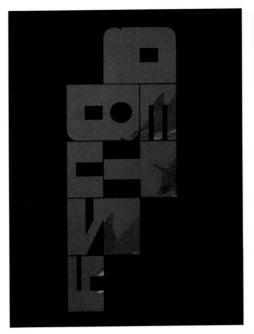

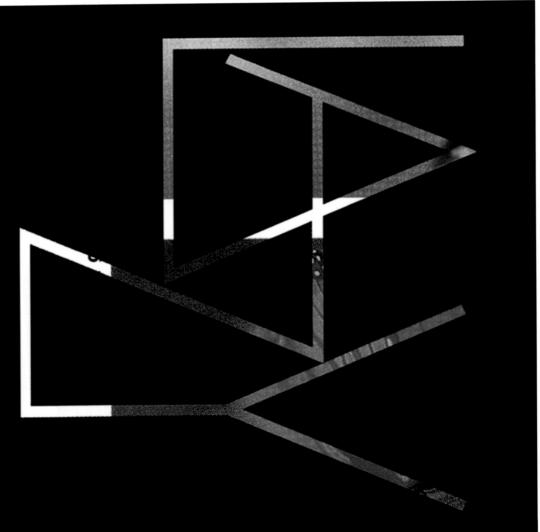

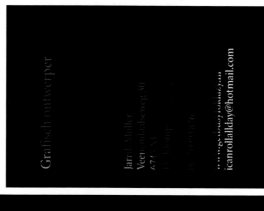

Grafisch ontwerper

Jarik Muller
Veenendaalseweg 30
674 NJ
Ilekkamp
t. 0655138876
www.getbusyfoklazy.nl
icanrollallday@hotmail.com

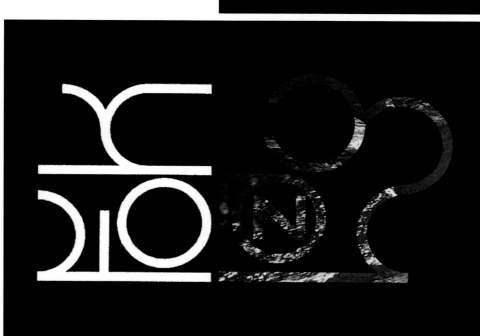

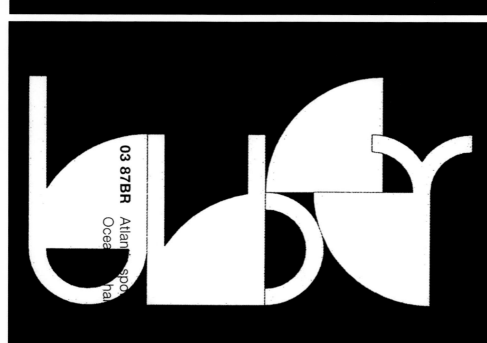

03 87BR

Atlant
Ocea
spo
ha

Design
Jarik Muller_
Get Busy Fok Lazy

For
Get Busy Fok Lazy_
Designer_
Amsterdam,
the Netherlands

Info
Taking pages from books and magazines, as well as advertising posters, Jarik Muller overprints elements of his constantly evolving logo, creating a dynamic series of large-scale cards (50x70mm/2x2.75in) that are never the same.

AMŒBACORP.

172 JOHN STREET, TORONTO ON CANADA M5T 1X5
TELEPHONE 416.599.2699 FACSIMILE 416.599.2391
WEBSITE AMOEBACORP.COM

CREATIVE DIRECTOR
MIKE KELAR EXT **308**
KELAR@AMOEBACORP.COM

Info
Using reclaimed billboard posters, environmentally certified papers and vegetable-based inks, AmoebaCorp produced a set of business cards and stationery employing die-cuts, two-colour printing and duplexing. Their aim, according to Mike Kelar, "was to find a responsible way of showcasing our position as agents of change… and recognize the amount of waste that designers create".

For
AmoebaCorp_
Designers_
Toronto, Canada

Design
Mike Kelar
Jayson Zaleski
Creative Direction
Mike Kelar
Mikey Richardson_
AmoebaCorp

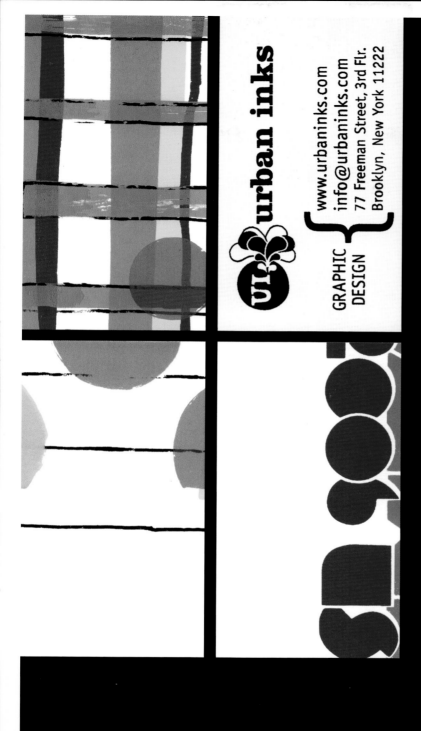

urban inks

www.urbaninks.com
info@urbaninks.com
77 Freeman Street, 3rd Flr.
Brooklyn, New York 11222

GRAPHIC DESIGN

Design
Reed Burgoyne_
Sarah Mead_
Urban Inks

For
Urban Inks_
Designers/
Screenprinting
Studio_
Brooklyn, USA

Info
From recycled test proofs (sheets used to prep the silk-screen, which are repeatedly overprinted) come interesting and unpredictable compositions. Urban Inks decided to utilize these as business cards by chopping them down and printing contact details on the reverse. Clients are invited to choose cards that best embody their perception of Urban Inks.

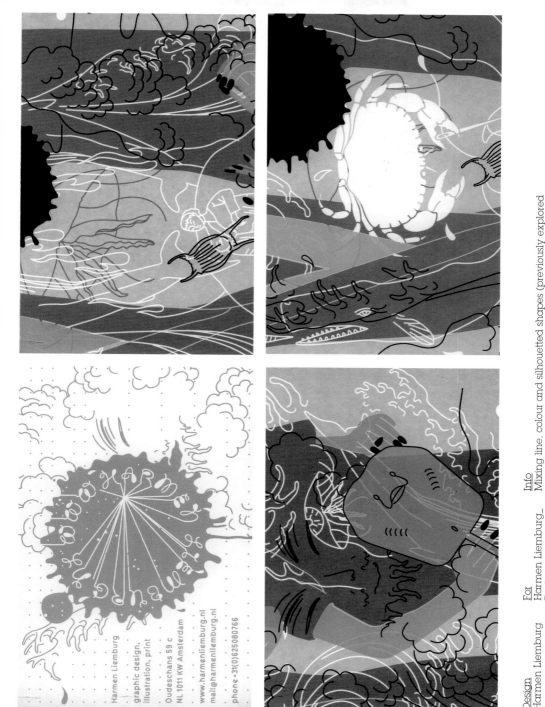

Harmen Liemburg

graphic design,
illustration, print

Oudeschans 59 c
NL 1011 KW Amsterdam

www.harmenliemburg.nl
mail@harmenliemburg.nl

phone +31(0)625080766

Design
Harmen Liemburg

For
Harmen Liemburg_
Designer_
Amsterdam,
the Netherlands

Info
Mixing line, colour and silhouetted shapes (previously explored
by Harmen Liemburg as fabric prints for Orson + Bodil) this set of
business cards is cut down from sheets of a four-colour silk-screen
print; the cropping process guarantees abstraction.

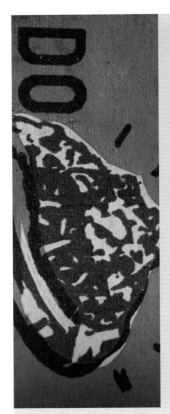

mwS

Matt Wingfield Studio Design/solutions

London
> 32 North Street, London, sw4 ohd
> t/f: 0207 720 2100 > m: 07775 787 031
> e: info@mattwingfieldstudio.com
> web: mattwingfieldstudio.com

Brighton
> Ground floor
> 42 a Providence Place,Brighton, bn1 4ge
> t/f: 01273 606 772

Design
Matt Wingfield_
Matt Wingfield
Studio – MWS

For
Matt Wingfield
Studio – MWS_
Designers_
London, UK

Info
Striving to keep craft skills alive in the field of design and illustration, Matt Wingfield loves silk-screen prints, rubber stamps, stencils, textures, found images, paper and card stocks. This is just a sample of an ongoing promotional project using hand-printed images as business cards and giveaways.

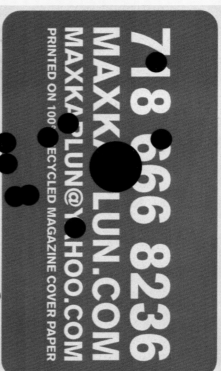

Design
Max Kaplun

For
Max Kaplun_
Designer_
Brooklyn, USA

Info
Making a virtue out of necessity, Max Kaplun overprints his contact details onto old covers of Metropolis, the New York design and architecture magazine. This tells us he's up to date with industry gossip, and that he's ecologically minded. The unpredictable results add an edge of excitement to the worthy proceedings.

Design
Fabian Monheim_
Fly Production

For
Fly Production_
Designers/
Art Directors/
Photographers_
London, UK

Info
Fabian Monheim likes to travel and set up shop around the world, which is why his business card doesn't include an address. Made from haptic paper, it is both tactile and techno; when embossed at exactly the right pressure and temperature it becomes alternately transparent and pigmented. "It's a very expensive process, so it's a good thing we didn't include the address as we're moving again!"

TOM CRAWSHAW

TOM CRAWSHAW

TOM CRAWSHAW

TOM CRAWSHAW

Tom Crawshaw
Graphic Designer

t +44 (0)7971 889692
e tom_crawshaw@hotmail.com
www.tomcrawshaw.co.uk

Design
Tom Crawshaw

For
Tom Crawshaw_
Designer_
Banbury, UK

Info
It couldn't be simpler. This one-colour, litho-printed card is left blank on the reverse for Tom Crawshaw to contact-print his logotype using a colour-coded rubber stamp. Every card is unique and no-nonsense – "akin to my approach to design", explains Crawshaw.

237

Anja Lutz // Book Design

Anja Lutz
Grafik Design(MA)
Choriner Str. 50
D-10435 Berlin
Tel.(030)275 96100
Fax(030)275 96101
anja@shift.de

Design
Anja Lutz

For
Anja Lutz_
Designer_
Berlin, Germany

Info
Book and magazine designer, not to mention self-publisher, Anja Lutz admits: "I easily grow tired of my own design identity and business card, and keep designing new ones." The rubber stamp and index card combination is a classic.

238

Design
David Bailey_
Kiosk

For
Kiosk_
Designer/
Art Director_
Sheffield, UK

Info
This sticker business card includes a "kiss cut" detail in the shape
of a speech bubble, allowing the logo to be lifted off and applied
to a range of surfaces for extra promo opportunities.

Design
Phil Bold_
Radford Wallis

For
Didde Thomsen-
Wasilewski_
Make-Up Artist_
Exeter, UK

Info
This clear-foiled, mirrorboard business card is super-sophisticated – and an imaginative design solution for a client in the beauty business.

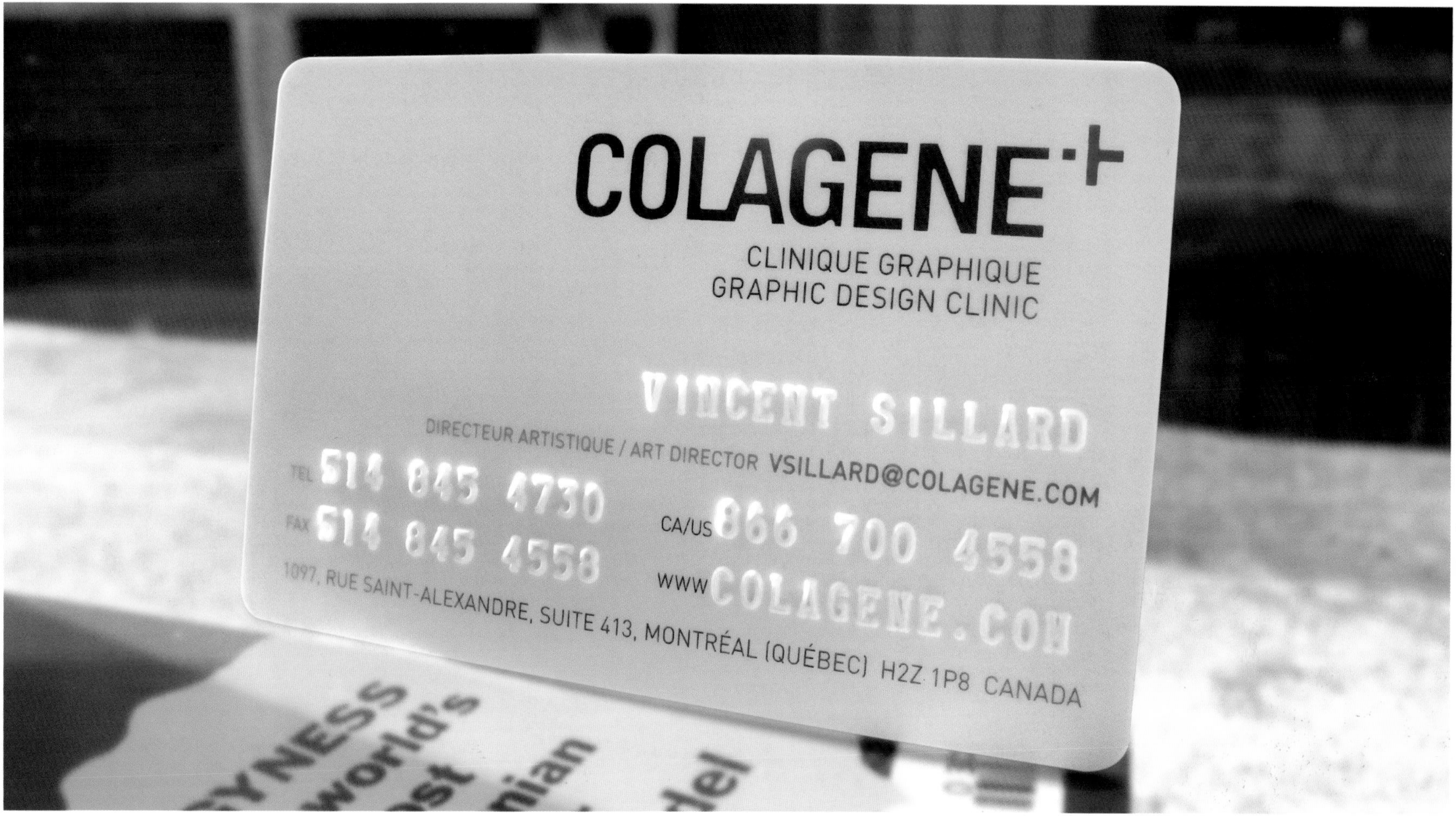

Design
Colagene

For
Colagene_
Designers_
Montreal,
Canada

Info
Borrowing the format of the Canadian "hospital card", which is a personal data file manufactured like a credit card, Colagene underline their "graphic design clinic" credentials – perfectly matching their contact details to the format.

Design
Paul Gray_
Suisse

For
Suisse_
Designer/
Art Director_
Glasgow, Scotland

Info
This double-sized business card uses its material and technique
– photo-etched metal – to good advantage. The logo is striped
and transparent so that it can be read from either side.

this is my card™

I am the creative director

this is my card™

CHRISTOPHER SIMMONS
cchris@minesf.com

I am the creative director

Design
Tim Belonax_
Christopher Simmons

Art Direction
Christopher Simmons
Mine™

For
Mine™_
Designers_
San Francisco, USA

Info
What could be simpler than black text on white card stock?
Add light and the magic of this business card is revealed, along
with the name and email address of the person behind the idea,
Christopher Simmons.

246

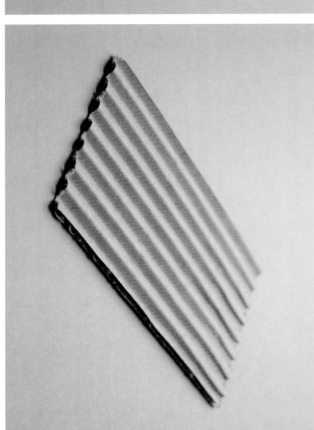

Design
Stephen Owen

For
Stephen Owen_
Designer_
Cheadle, UK

Info
Take corrugated card, with its distinctive buff colour and grainy texture, and add a one-colour screenprint in mint green. The result is timeless, no-nonsense and stand-out.

hatch

Katie Jain
katie@hatchsf.com
Principal / Creative Director

353 Broadway Street
San Francisco CA 94133

HATCH DESIGN LLC

hatch

Joel Templin
jtemplin@hatchsf.com
Principal / Creative Director

353 Broadway Street
San Francisco CA 94133

HATCH DESIGN LLC

T 415 398 1650
F 415 398 1660

Design
Eszter Clark
Creative Direction
Katie Jain_
Joel Templin_
Hatch Design

For
Hatch Design_
Designers_
San Francisco, USA

Info
Since they're called Hatch, it made sense to use egg-carton material for their business cards. Going straight to the manufacturer, they had to wait until a farm requested a large order, and then got 500 flat sheets of card from the run. The board is foil-stamped with the logo, and an area is debossed for the sticker. Printed offset in the company colours of blue and orange, the stickers are then engraved with each staff member's contact details.

Bethan Laura Wood
07754064070
heinzmeanzbeanz@yahoo.co.uk
www.woodlondon.co.uk

Design
Bethan Wood_
Wood London

Typography
Hugo Frost

Laser-Cutting
Tamatec

For
Wood London_
Product and
Jewellery Designer_
London, UK

Info
This innovative young product designer set out to explore the potential of laser-cutting 3mm (0.125in) plywood. The results included a range of jewellery and a business card. "It's designed to be kept," explains Bethan Wood, "and to be reminiscent of the work I do."

VIC
POLKINGHORNE

CREATIVE DIRECTOR

SELL! SELL!
8 PRINTING HOUSE YARD,
HACKNEY ROAD, LONDON E2 7PR
TELEPHONE 0207 0333 999
MOBILE 07930 386669
EMAIL VIC@SELLSELL.CO.UK
VISIT SELLSELL.CO.UK

THIS CARD
brings the holder
GOOD LUCK

SELL! SELL!

Design
Vic Polkinghorne_
Sell Sell!

For
Sell Sell_
Creative Agency_
London, UK

Info
Using recycled board and vegetable inks, this set of business cards presents the tongue-in-cheek wit of a creative agency, while demonstrating that you can have maximum fun and green credentials.

Judith Wilding
Creative Director

Delicious Industries
1, 36 First Avenue
Hove BN3 2FF

T: 01273 820799
M: 07754 729960
E: judith@deliciousindustries.com
W: deliciousindustries.com

Design
Judith Wilding_
Delicious Industries

For
Delicious Industries_
Designers_
Hove, UK

Info
A cost-effective and environmentally friendly business card is printed using vegetable inks and packing board. By combining the rough with the smooth in the form of a heraldic crest and a calligraphic flourish, this card hints at grander things.

MICHI KERN

LEDERERSTR. 3
80331 MÜNCHEN
FON: +49 89 23 23 91 91
FAX: +49 89 23 23 91 92
MOBIL: 0172 / 28 53 67 0
EMAIL: MICHI@ZERWIRK.DE
WWW.ZERWIRK.DE

Design
Christian
Hundertmark_
C100 Studio

For
Zerwirk_
Restaurant/Bar/
Club_
Munich, Germany

Info
To promote this hip vegan restaurant that doubles as a cultural
hub, housing a bar, club, events and exhibitions, Christian
Hundertmark created a business card using tactile grey board,
contemporary typography and elegant illustrative elements.

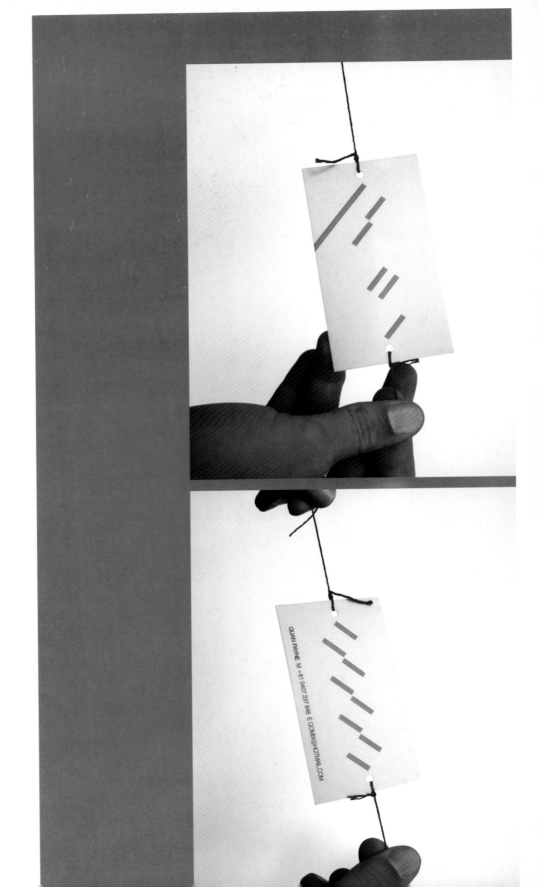

Design
Quan Payne

For
Quan Payne_
Designer_
Sydney, Australia

Info
By printing some seemingly abstract shapes on both sides of this uncoated stock, then hand-punching two holes and threading lengths of red string, Quan Payne created a truly interactive business card that "allows the user to discover a hidden message through play and lateral thought".

256

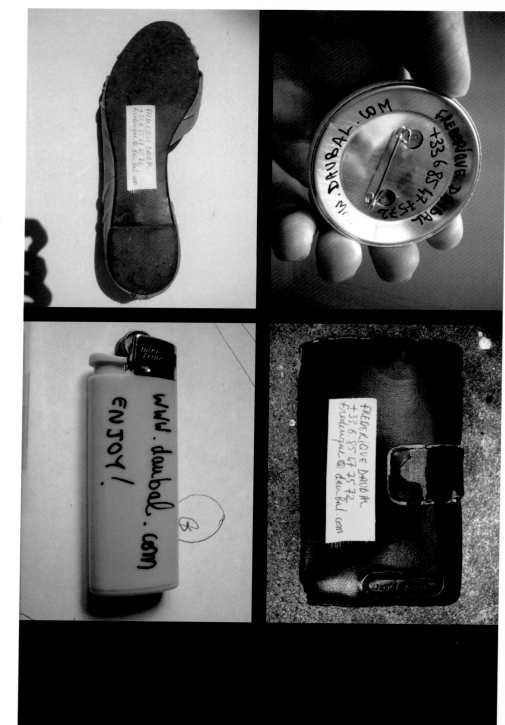

Design
Frederique Daubal_
Daubal

For
Daubal_
Designer_
Paris, France

Info
Described as an "action card", whenever Daubal needs to give a person her contact details she whips out the permanent black marker she always carries and writes "something personal on whatever material I manage to find; that way it's quite spontaneous, unique and just for them."

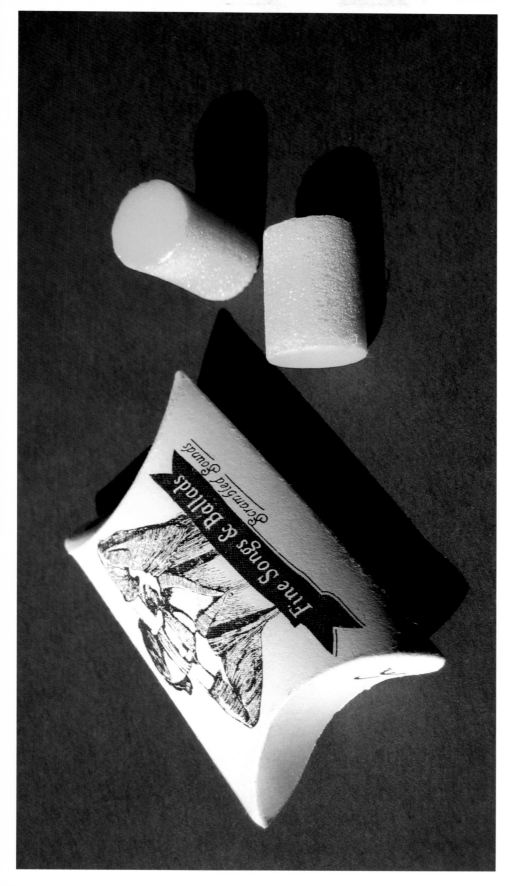

Design
Sam Harris

For
Scrambled Sounds_
DJ Collective
Burgess Hill, UK

Info
This laser-printed hand-made box, which contains a pair of earplugs, is "a tongue-in-cheek approach to please my next-door neighbours," says Sam Harris, designer and DJ.

Fine Songs & Ballads
Scrambled Sounds

258

Design
Chin-Lien Chen_
Chris Vermaas_
Office of CC

For
De Kunstrijders_
Art Transporters_
Amsterdam,
the Netherlands

Info
A pre-printed "luggage label", complete with cord tie, tear-off "notes" section and a "seal of approval" driver logo on an accompanying envelope, this business card is the definition of bells and whistles. Each card is printed with a unique serial number and may be attached directly to the artwork being transported, functioning as an inventory/identity marker. Meanwhile, witty copy – "We drive for…. Picasso, Pollock, Rembrandt, Rodin…" – drops some reassuring names.

BEDRIJFSNAAM

DE KUNSTRIJDERS

STRAAT QUELLIJNSTRAAT 109

POSTCODE NL-1073XH

STAD AMSTERDAM

TELEFOON 020.679.6378

MOBIEL +31.(0)6.40.29.83.38

FACSIMILE 084.223.4293

E-MAIL JOOST@DEKUNSTRIJD

WEBSITE WWW

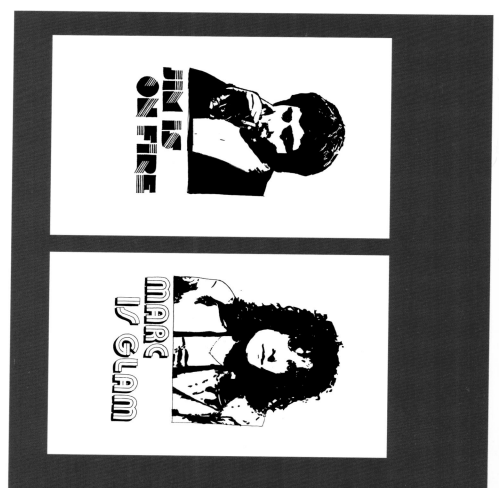

LOU IS WILD

OZZY IS MY IDOL

KEITH IS STONED

LEMMY LIKES GIRLS

Design
Rose Stallard

For
Lookinshifty_
Illustrator_
London, UK

Info
Rose Stallard, aka Lookinshifty, is renowned for her renditions of musical bad boys, and has a fascination with the graphic language, logos and equipment of rock and roll. Here, among other things, she reuses one of popular music's perennial promo items, the guitar plectrum, as a business card.

Design
Bunch

For
Chokolate_
Casting Agency
and Dance Studio_
London, UK

Info
A chocolate and cream identity, bearing the tag line "mmm",
was created for an agency that prides itself on nurturing talent
for the entertainment industry. The business cards are wrapped
in gold foil, necessitating audience participation, and the
anticipation of a lovely surprise – "mmm" …

Design
Blackbooks

For
Firestone/
Dustin Orlando_
Entertainment
Agency_
Orlando, USA

Info
This card borrows an icon from the 1980s. Mr T combined style, strength and attitude, as well as a lot of bling… perfect for a club promoter.

Info
This death's-head, beret-wearing, beatnik Mickey
defines PTC as part of the "alt-Orlando" community.

For
PTC Orlando_
Promotional
Agency_
Orlando, USA

Design
Blackbooks_
Paul Geller

BLACKBOOKSTENCILS.COM

Design
Blackbooks

For
Blackbooks,
Creative Agency
and Laser
Fabrication_
Miami, USA

Info
This unique creative agency offers specialist technical advice and laser-cutting and engraving in a range of materials, including matboard and plywood, ideal for stencilling. Working with renowned artists, they also stage installations and exhibitions. Blackbooks are major players on the Miami art scene and produce a range of high-profile business cards for themselves and clients.

Design
Katie Jain_
Joel Templin_
Hatch Design

For
JAQK Cellars_
Wine Brand_
San Francisco, USA

Info
Setting up a sideline company isn't a new idea for designers. Going into the wine business is a little unusual, though, so Katie Jain and Joel Templin decided to deploy their design skills fully. "JAQK Cellars is dedicated to two things: making great wine, and something we all love, play," Templin explains. "JAQK stands for Jack, Ace, Queen, King, so the business cards are minted and coined metal in the style of poker chips."

Mike's Studio_
mikesstudio.co.uk

Mine™_
minesf.com

Morten Laursen_
mortenlaursen.com

Neil McFarland_
parishall.com

No Days Off_
nodaysoff.com

Office of CC_
ver-xs4all.nl

Omar Vulpinari_
ovulpinari@alice.it

One Lucky Guitar, Inc._
oneluckyguitar.com

PetPunk_
petpunk.com

Phil Bold_
mbold@philbold.com

Purple Haze Studio_
thepurplehaze.net

Quan Payne_
quanpayne.com

RC_
arcee.nl

Revenge Is Sweet_
revengeissweet.org

Richard Hogg_
hi099.com

Rose Stallard_
rosestallard.com
breedlondon.com

Sabine Kobel_
sabinekobel.com

Sam Green_
samgreenwork.com

Sam Harris_
samtriptych.co.uk

Sarah Boris_
sarah.boris@gmail.com

Scrollan_
scrollan.de

Sell! Sell!_
sellsell.co.uk

Serial Cut™_
serialcut.com

Simone Wagener_
simonewagener.com

Space150_
space150.com

Start Creative_
startcreative.co.uk

Stephen Owen_
stephenowen.co.uk

Sterk Water_
sterkwater.be

Steven Wilson_
wilson2000.com
breedlondon.com

Stiletto NYC_
stilettonyc.com

Studio Charvéz_
studiocharvez.com

Studio8 Design_
studio8design.co.uk

Studio Lonne Wennekendonk_
lonnewennekendonk.nl

Studio Output_
studio-output.com

Suisse_
suissestudio.com

Telemetre_
telemetre.net

Theresa Vandling_
vandling.co.uk

Thirteen_
thirteen.co.uk

This Is Crap_
thisiscrap.org

This Studio-
this-studio.co.uk

Tom Crawshaw_
tomcrawshaw.co.uk

Tom Mesquitta_
mesquitta@mac.com

Trickel_
trickel.net

Ulla Puggaard_
up@ullapuggaard.com
tomorrowmanagement.com

Urban Inks_
urbaninks.com

Vonsung_
vonsung.com

Wood London_
woodlondon.co.uk